A WALKING TOUR
LONDON

Sketches of the city's architectural treasures

Journey through Lond

T0166752

SECOND EDITION

Gregory Byrne Bracken

Marshall Cavendish
Editions

Text and illustrations by Gregory Byrne Bracken
Book design by Benson Tan

Copyright © 2019, 2011 Marshall Cavendish International (Asia) Pte Ltd

First published in 2011

Second edition published in 2019 by Marshall Cavendish Editions
An imprint of Marshall Cavendish International

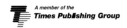

Other Marshall Cavendish Offices:
Marshall Cavendish Corporation, 99 White Plains Road, Tarrytown NY 10591-9001,
USA • Marshall Cavendish International (Thailand) Co Ltd, 253 Asoke, 12th Flr,
Sukhumvit 21 Road, Klongtoey Nua, Wattana, Bangkok 10110, Thailand • Marshall
Cavendish (Malaysia) Sdn Bhd, Times Subang, Lot 46, Subang Hi-Tech Industrial
Park, Batu Tiga, 40000 Shah Alam, Selangor Darul Ehsan, Malaysia.

Marshall Cavendish is a registered trademark of Times Publishing Limited

National Library Board, Singapore Cataloguing-in-Publication Data

Name(s): Byrne Bracken, G. (Gregory).
Title: London : A Walking Tour / Gregory Byrne Bracken.
Description: Second edition. | Singapore : Marshall Cavendish Editions, 2019. |
Includes index. | First published: 2011.
Identifier(s): OCN 1104213758 | ISBN 978-981-4841-91-7 (paperback)
Subject(s): LCSH: Walking–England–London–Guidebooks. | Historic buildings–
England–London–Guidebooks. | Historic sites–England–London–Guidebooks. |
London (England)–Tours. | London (England)–Guidebooks.
Classification: DDC 914.21–dc23

Printed in Singapore

For Robert Cortlever

CONTENTS

Acknowledgments

I would like thank Melvin Neo and Justin Lau at Marshall Cavendish,
who have been such a pleasure to work with over the years. I also want
to thank my cousin Nicholas Bracken OBE for showing me the city
he was lucky enough to call home when I was an intern in
London in the 1980s.

Introduction

One of the world's greatest cities, London was also the capital of the British Empire – the largest empire the world has ever seen. Founded by another empire, the Roman, around 50 CE, the city experienced steady growth over the millennia until the 19th century, when its size and population simply exploded. It has had its fair share of setbacks as well – invasions, plagues, the Great Fire of 1666. The city has been the birthplace of some truly remarkable innovations in architecture, from Inigo Jones's majestic Banqueting House to Christopher Wren's stunning dome on St Paul's Cathedral, as well as more recent innovations like Richard Rogers's futuristic Lloyd's of London.

Despite its huge size, London divides rather neatly into districts. The walks in this book cover each of them in turn, starting with the oldest – Spitalfields and the City of London. Each of the 13 walks starts where the previous one left off, while the final chapters cover places that are a little out of town, such as Hampstead, Greenwich, Kew Gardens and Hampton Court Palace. The various architectural styles and features mentioned in the book are explained at the end.

All that remains is for you to enjoy your time walking around this most aristocratic yet accessible of cities.

History

London is the capital of the United Kingdom. Called Londinium when it was first founded by the Romans around 50 CE, it occupied an area roughly the size of Hyde Park (250 hectares, or 625 acres). By the 2nd century, Londinium had replaced Colchester as the capital of Roman Britain, and its population had reached 60,000. It boasted a number of important buildings, including the largest basilica north of the Alps, as well as temples, bath houses and an amphitheatre. Between 190 and 225 CE the Romans built the London Wall. The 3-kilometre wall defined the city's perimeter for the next 1,600 years; six of its seven gates are Roman: Ludgate, Newgate, Aldersgate, Cripplegate, Bishopsgate and Aldgate (Moorgate is medieval). In 410 CE Roman rule ceased in Britain and the city experienced a rapid decline.

An Anglo-Saxon settlement is believed to have then grown up to the west of the old Roman walls, dating from the end of the 5th century. The population was as high as 12,000 people at this time. By 650 CE, it had become Christian.

Vikings from Denmark attacked the city throughout the 9th and 10th centuries, with English resistance finally collapsing in 1013. Rival Danish claimants fought for the throne, with King Canute finally defeating Edmund Ironside to gain control of all of England north of the Thames (which included London). Edmund's death a few weeks later left Canute in control of the whole country.

English rule was restored by Edward the Confessor in 1042 after the extinction of Canute's dynasty. The new king founded Westminster Abbey and established Westminster as the centre of government; it proved to be a serious rival to the power of the old City of London. Edward's death in 1066 left England open to Norman invasion, with William the Bastard, Duke of Normandy, defeating King Harold at the Battle of Hastings later that year.

The first thing that William the Conqueror did was build a new fortress on the Thames. The Tower of London was one of the first stone castles to be built in England and King William granted a charter confirming the City of London's existing rights, privileges and laws in 1067. The City's powers of self-government would be increased significantly under King John at the beginning of the 13th century. The Palace of Westminster was built in the 11th century, followed by London Bridge in the 1170s. Trade grew steadily throughout the Middle Ages, and the city grew rapidly; by 1300 the population was around 80,000. London lost half its population during the plague known as the Black Death in the middle of the 14th century, but made a rapid recovery.

Under the Tudors, who reigned from 1485 to 1603, England turned to Protestantism. Up to this point over half the land in London was owned by monasteries, nunneries or other religious establishments. With Henry VIII's dissolution of the monasteries in 1536, however, almost all of this valuable property changed hands. London had also become an important commercial centre, with trade expanding beyond Europe to Russia, the Holy Land and the Americas. Companies such as the East India Company were established – the first steps towards the establishment of the vast British Empire. The 16th and early 17th centuries were remarkably rich not just in terms of material wealth but also culturally. British drama enjoyed a golden age under Elizabeth I, with playwrights such as Christopher Marlowe, Ben Jonson, and above all, William Shakespeare.

Telephone box

By this time, London had expanded beyond the boundaries of the old City, as aristocrats with business at the royal court began to live in the West End. This was the beginning of the 'London season', which saw urban development in places like Lincoln's Inn Fields (1629) and the Piazza of Covent Garden (1632, designed by Inigo Jones).

London suffered a double blow in the mid-1660s. The Great Plague of 1665 killed about one-fifth of the population, and the following year the Great Fire destroyed about 60 percent of the city's built fabric. (The fire in a way proved helpful – eradicating the last of the plague.) Within a few days of the fire, plans were presented by Christopher Wren, John Evelyn and Robert Hooke for the rebuilding of the city. Wren was given the job of rebuilding the City's churches, including St Paul's Cathedral; Hooke oversaw the reconstruction of the City's houses.

By the end of the 17th century, the City of London had supplanted Amsterdam as the world's financial capital. The Bank of England was founded in 1694 and by 1700 London was handling 80 percent of England's imports, 69 percent of exports and 86 percent of re-exports. Many of these goods were luxuries from the Americas and Asia: silk, sugar, tea, tobacco. William III disliked London, so he, along with his wife Mary II, developed Kensington Palace, which began to draw London's growth westwards. The establishment of Greenwich Hospital also extended the city to the east and south.

In 1707 the Act of Union merged the Scottish and English parliaments to establish the Kingdom of Great Britain. Throughout the 18th century, immigration boosted the city's population, while military and naval victories enhanced London's global standing. The year 1750 saw the opening of Westminster Bridge, up till which time the only way across the Thames was by London Bridge or ferry. George III bought Buckingham House in 1762, and over the next 75 years, with the help of architects like John Nash, turned it into a palace. It was also during this time that London's great Georgian squares were laid out.

During the 19th century, the city's population grew from 1 million to 6.7 million. London was the capital of the British Empire, as well as the world's political, financial and cultural capital. But alongside the lavish wealth there was a city of dire poverty – as immortalised in the novels of Charles Dickens. The railway arrived at this time, linking the city with the rest of the country; the termini were housed in magnificent new station buildings, like Euston and St Pancras. London was the first city in the world to develop an underground rail system, which allowed people to commute from their homes at the edges of the ever-expanding metropolis. One of the most notable events of the century was the Great Exhibition of 1851, where the magnificent Crystal Palace – a marvel of 19th-century engineering – showcased Britain to the world.

London in 1900 was a city at the height of its global dominance. World War I, however, dealt a shattering blow, significantly undermining the confidence and faith in the political system that had made Britain great. This was further compounded by the Great Depression of the 1930s and the hardships of World War II. From September 1940 to May 1941 the Blitz laid waste to huge swathes of the city, including many of its beloved landmarks. This was undoubtedly devastating, but it was also, in many ways, London's finest hour, for the city's indomitable spirit survived. The failure of the German invasion turned the tide of the war and led to the eventual victory for the Allies in 1945.

London's recovery was slow, in spite of events such as the 1948 Summer Olympics and the 1951 Festival of Britain. It was not helped by the fact that the once-great empire vanished almost overnight – a serious psychological blow for the former imperial capital. And the city was in a shambles. Well-meaning attempts to rehouse the population had led architects to build ghastly tower blocks in a botched reinterpretation of Modernist ideals.

It wasn't until the 1960s that a remarkable renaissance in the city's confidence and cultural importance took place – when it became the epicentre for new movements in fashion, music and the arts. Carnaby Street and Abbey Road (with its famous recording studios) became household names the world over. The role of London as a trendsetter for youth culture has continued ever since, from the Punk movement of the 1970s, through the New Wave of the 80s and the Cool Britannia of the 90s. The 1980s also saw the deregulation of the financial markets in the City of London – known as the Big Bang – which did much to re-establish London as a major global financial centre, a role it had lost out to cities like New York and Tokyo.

London in the 21st century is a place that treasures its history. It is possible to visit Roman, medieval, Georgian, Victorian and 20th-century buildings, sometimes all in one small area. But London is also a city that looks to the future, with projects like the Millennium Dome at Greenwich (a remarkable feat of engineering even if aesthetically polarising), and the London Eye, both designed to usher in the new millennium. A stroll through London's streets is a stroll though two millennia of architectural history. All that remains is for you to enjoy that history as you make your way around one of the world's most spectacular architectural treasure houses.

Climate

London has a temperate maritime climate which rarely experiences extremes of temperature. Central London can be as much as 5°C warmer than surrounding areas. Summers are generally warm, with daytime temperatures in the range of 20–25°C (68–77°F), and rarely above 30°C (86°F). Winters are cold but rarely freezing, daytime temperatures in the range of 6–8°C (43–46°F). Snow, while uncommon, does fall in the city during the winter. Spring is typically mild and cool; it is also the driest season of the year. Autumn is usually mild too, but can be unsettled, with temperatures hovering around the 18°C (64°F) mark until the end of September. Despite England's reputation for rain, London is a relatively dry city, with generally light, albeit regular, precipitation throughout the year.

Suggested Itineraries

Roman architecture
Smithfield: Museum of London
The City: Old Roman wall

Medieval architecture
Smithfield
The City
Southwark
Holborn

Georgian architecture
St James's
Bloomsbury
Regent's Park
Further Afield: Hampstead, Greenwich and Kew Gardens

Victorian architecture
The City
Westminster
Kensington (museums)

20th-century architecture
The City
South Bank

Parks and gardens
St James's
Regent's Park
Kensington: Hyde Park and Kensington Gardens
Chelsea: Battersea Park
Further Afield: Hampstead, Greenwich and Kew Gardens

Panoramic views
South Bank: London Eye
Further Afield: Hampstead and Greenwich

Shopping and markets
Smithfield
Southwark
Soho
Covent Garden
Kensington
Chelsea

Nightlife
Soho
Covent Garden

Children's
Bloomsbury: Pollack's Toy Museum
Regent's Park: London Zoo, Madame Tussauds
Further Afield: Kew Gardens

Key to Icons

 Must See

 National Monument

 Good View

 See At Night

 Drinking

 Eating

 Shopping

Map of London

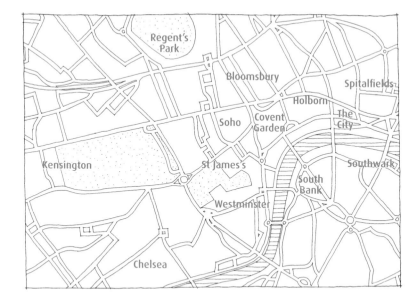

Spitalfields

Nearest Tube: Aldgate
Approximate walking time: 2 hours 30 minutes

Spitalfields

The rather odd-sounding name of Spitalfields comes from the priory of St Mary Spital located here in medieval times. This district is among the oldest and most historic in London, with one of the city's oldest churches, a number of Jacobean houses, as well as the remains of the city's Roman wall. The area is also a mecca for shoppers, with Petticoat Lane (for clothes), Brick Lane (for spicy Bengali food), and Old Smithfield Market – the sole survivor of central London's once-numerous wholesale food markets. To the west lies Smithfield, where peasant rebel Wat Tyler was killed in 1381, protesting Richard II's high taxes; later, during the reign of Bloody Mary (Mary I), scores of martyrs were burned at the stake here for being Protestant. Smithfield's meat market was established on this ancient execution site – safely outside the old city walls.

SPITALFIELDS

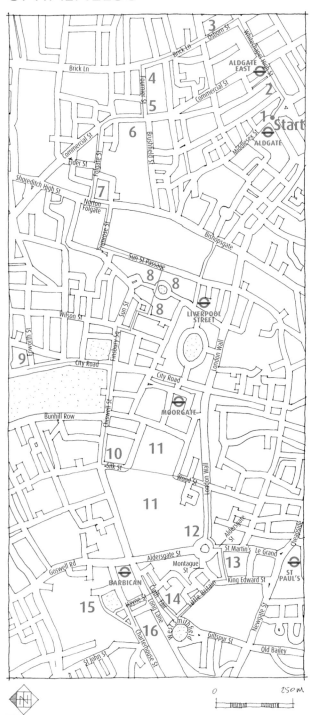

Brick Ln

3

Osborn St

Brick Ln

ALDGATE
EAST

Fournier St

4

Commercial St

2

5

1

Start

6

Brushfield St

Middlesex St

ALDGATE

Commercial St

Elder St

Folgate St

Shoreditch High St

7

Norton
Folgate

Wilmore St

Bishopsgate

Sun St Passage

8

8

Sun St

8

Wilson St

Finsbury St

LIVERPOOL
STREET

Edworth St

London Wall

9

City Road

City Road

Finsbury St

MOORGATE

Bunhill Row

10

11

Silk St

London Wall

Wood St

11

12

Aldersgate St

St Martin's Le Grand

Cheapside

Aldersgate St

Montague
St

13

Goswell Rd

BARBICAN

King Edward St

ST
PAUL'S

Hayne St

14

Little Britain

15

Long Lane

Newgate St

16

Smithfield

Giltspur St

Old Bailey

St John St

Charterhouse St

N

0   250 M

16

KEY

1. Petticoat Lane
2. Whitechapel Gallery
3. Brick Lane
4. Fournier Street
5. Christ Church, Spitalfields
6. Old Spitalfields Market
7. Dennis Severs's House
8. Broadgate Centre
9. Wesley's Chapel
10. Whitbread's Brewery
11. Barbican
12. Museum of London
13. St Botolph's, Aldersgate
14. St Bartholomew-the-Great
15. Charterhouse
16. Smithfield Market

Petticoat Lane ❶

Leave Aldgate station, and Middlesex Street – the official name of Petticoat Lane – will be at the junction of Aldgate High Street, Whitechapel High Street and St Botolph Street. A bustling clothes market is held here every Sunday morning. This has grown over the years and spread over surrounding streets, notably Wentworth Street, which has a market every day except Saturday, the Jewish sabbath – which reflects the Jewish character that the area had in the 19th century. The market experienced a decline after World War II but was revitalised from the 1970s by Asian immigrants, particularly Indians and Bangladeshis. Many good-quality, cheap places to eat South Asian food are located here, and there are also still a few specialising in traditional Jewish food. Numerous attempts were made to close the market down over the years before it was finally safeguarded by an act of parliament in 1936. Called Hog's Lane in the Middle Ages, it was renamed Middlesex Street during Queen Victoria's reign, but the more colourful nickname Petticoat Lane seems to have stuck.

Petticoat Lane
Opening times: 9am–2pm Sun; admission free

Whitechapel Gallery ❷

Return to Whitechapel High Street and turn left; the Whitechapel Gallery will be on your left. This delightful sandstone building, with its striking asymmetrical facade, was designed by Charles Harrison Townsend in 1895 and built between 1897 and 1899. It was founded with the aim of bringing art to the people of East London. In the 1950s and '60s it exhibited the works of such international luminaries as Jackson Pollock, Robert Rauschenberg, Anthony Caro and John Hoyland, and in 1970 David Hockney held his debut exhibition here.

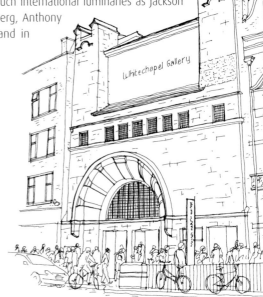

Recently expanded, the gallery continues to maintain its reputation for high-quality exhibitions and serve as the centre of the area's burgeoning arts scene – thus fulfilling its original brief. As one might expect, there is a well-stocked bookshop, and a café, which serves a range of wholesome food in a relaxed atmosphere.

Whitechapel Gallery

Whitechapel Gallery
Opening times: 11am–6pm Tue–Sun (to 9pm Thur)
Admission free
www.whitechapel.org
Tel: 020-7522 7888

> **Did You Know?**
> The Whitechapel Gallery temporarily hosted Pablo Picasso's masterpiece *Guernica* in 1938 as part of a travelling exhibition to protest the Spanish Civil War.

Brick Lane ❸

Continue along Whitechapel High Street and turn left onto Osborn Street, which turns into Brick Lane after a short distance. In the 19th century this was the heart of London's Jewish district and is named for a laneway that used to run through the city's brickfields. Some Jewish businesses remain, including a bagel shop at No. 159. The area is now home to London's Bengali community; the air is pungent with spices, and sari-clad women rustle past shops selling South Asian food, clothes, and Bengali movies, the sounds of which blast out into the street.

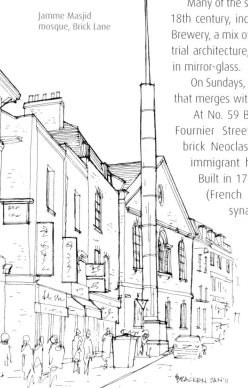

Jamme Masjid
mosque, Brick Lane

Many of the shops and houses date from the 18th century, including the former Black Eagle Brewery, a mix of 18th- and 19th-century industrial architecture, with a recent extension clad in mirror-glass.

On Sundays, Brick Lane hosts a large market that merges with nearby Petticoat Lane.

At No. 59 Brick Lane, on the corner with Fournier Street, stands a simple brown-brick Neoclassical building. It reflects the immigrant history of the area perfectly. Built in 1743 as a chapel for Huguenots (French Protestants), it became a synagogue in the 19th century, then a Methodist chapel in the early 20th century. It is now a mosque, the **Jamme Masjid**, reflecting the area's most recent but surely not last wave of immigrants.

Brick Lane Market
Hours: 9am–5pm Sun
Admission free

Fournier Street ❹

The houses on this pretty little street date from the 1720s and form one of the most important and best preserved collections of early Georgian domestic architecture in the country. Built for French Huguenot silk-weavers, the houses were fitted with wood panelling, carved staircases and fireplaces, as well as decorative doors.

Howard House, at No. 14, is one of the finest. It was built around 1726 and leased to the weavers Signeratt and Bourdillon; the loom was kept in the attic because this would have been the room with the best light. No. 23 is a superb example of a single-fronted early Georgian townhouse in the city. Its simple, elegant design retains the original arrangement of three storeys over a basement, and a mansard attic with windows wide enough to allow in maximum light for weaving. The artists Gilbert and George lived and worked on this street for a number of years, and featured the interior of their house in a number of their works – they show a gloomy and dilapidated house from the 1970s (a low point in London for the appreciation of Georgian architecture).

Fournier Street's textile tradition continues to this day in the form of immigrant labourers – Bengali rather than Huguenot – toiling away on sewing machines.

Christ Church, Spitalfields ❺

At the end of Fournier Street is Christ Church, Spitalfields. Commissioned by parliament under the Fifty New Churches Act of 1711 (the purpose of which was to combat the threat of non-conformism to the Church of England), Christ Church, Spitalfields is a strong architectural statement; it was also one that was needed in this particular part of the city because of the influence of the Huguenot silk-weavers who had flooded into the area after escaping religious persecution in France.

Widely regarded as the finest of Nicholas Hawksmoor's six London churches, this English Baroque masterpiece still dominates its surroundings. The majestic portico and spire are best seen from the far end of Brushfield Street. The interior's impression of power and grandeur is reinforced by its high ceiling and the sturdy wooden canopy over the west door and gallery. Alterations during the Victorian era nearly destroyed Hawksmoor's design – the Victorians having a penchant for giving older, plainer churches a makeover, turning many a chaste facade into the 19th-century equivalent of mutton dressed as lamb – but recent restorations have returned this church to its original beauty.

Christ Church, Spitalfields
Opening times: 10am–4pm Mon–Fri; 1–4pm Sun
Admission free (charges for guided tours)
www.spitalfieldsvenue.org
Tel: 020-7377 6793

Christ Church, Spitalfields

Old Spitalfields Market ⑥

London's oldest market is a charming, gabled, red-brick building diagonally across Commercial Street from Christ Church, Spitalfields. Its large halls were roofed over in glass by the architects Foster and Partners when it was renovated in 2005. This award-winning market is housed in a building that dates from the end of the 19th century, although the market itself started way back in 1682. Open seven days a week, the market is liveliest on Sundays. On offer is a wide variety of fashions – from cutting-edge young designers to vintage clothing – original artworks, crafts, jewellery, furnishings, children's toys. There are also plenty of food shops and restaurants as well as places to buy organic fruit and vegetables, bread and preserves.

Old Spitalfields Market
Opening times: 10am–8pm Mon–Fri; 10am–6pm Sat; 10am–5pm Sun
(Thur: antiques market; Fri: fashion and art market)
Admission free
www.oldspitalfieldsmarket.com

Dennis Severs's House ⑦

Continue up Commercial Street and turn left onto Folgate Street. On the right, **Elder Street** has two of London's earliest surviving terraces, with several sensitively restored Georgian red-brick houses. Continue along Folgate Street and you will come to Dennis Severs's House on your left at No. 18.

This is one of the most remarkable museums in London. American designer and performer Dennis Severs (1948–1999) was a confirmed Anglophile, but what was unusual about his love of all things British was the desire to live as if it was still the reign of George III – something that would have sat well with the English love of eccentricity. This charming house, built in 1724, has been preserved in that manner – heated by fireplaces and lit by candlelight. To add to the sense of time-travel, recordings of atmospheric sounds are played throughout the museum: the rustling of silk dresses, the clatter of hooves on the cobbles outside. Meticulously staged to show the home life of a fictitious Huguenot silk-weaver, the rooms look as if the occupants have simply stepped out for a moment – there is bread on the plates and wine in the glasses. The décor also reflects the changes that would have taken place over the years, and it this mix of 18th- and 19th-century styles that gives the museum the feel of a real home.

Dennis Severs's House
Opening times: Noon–4pm Sun; noon–2pm Mon; 5–9pm Mon, Wed, Fri
Admission charges
www.dennissevershouse.co.uk
Tel: 020-7247 4013

Broadgate Centre

Turn left at the end of Folgate Street and you will be on Shoreditch High Street; take a right onto Primrose Street and then a left onto Old Broad Street; **Exchange Square** will be on your left. Created in the 1990s as part of the Liverpool Street railway station redevelopment, this square commands wonderful views of the glass-roofed train shed – the terminus for trains from eastern England. Unfortunately, it does not make for such a wonderful view itself, consisting as it does of typical late 20th-century commercial hodge-podge architecture that in trying to look impressive only manages to bury itself in banality.

Dennis Severs's House

Across from Old Broad Street sits the massive Broadgate Centre, a 13-hectare (32-acre) office and retail complex built between 1985 and 1991, the largest office development in London until Canary Wharf in the early 1990s. It consists of a sequence of squares – each with its own distinctive character – the largest of which, Broadgate Arena, is used as an entertainment venue. Rising above the centre is the 164-metre (538-foot) Broadgate Tower. Broadgate Centre also features a number of art works – including Richard Serra's *Fulcrum*, George Segal's *Rush Hour Group* and Barry Flanagan's *Leaping Hare on Crescent and Bell* – and, since 2010, a twice-monthly farmers' market.

Wesley's Chapel ❾

Leave Broadgate Centre via Sun Street and cross Finsbury Square to get to City Road. Wesley's Chapel, also known as the Leysian Mission, will be on your right after Epworth Street. John Wesley was the founder of the Methodist church and laid the foundation stone of the chapel in 1777. Sparely decorated, this would have reflected Wesley's austere religious principles. Some of the columns were made from ships' masts. Wesley preached here until his death in 1791 and is buried behind the chapel. A museum explains the history of the Methodist faith. Also included in this small but charming enclave is the house in which Wesley lived. It is still possible to see some of his furniture and books.

Across City Road from Wesley's Chapel lies **Bunhill Fields**, a cemetery that dates from the time of the Great Plague of 1665. Twenty years later it was allocated for use by Non-conformists, who were banned from burial in Church of England churchyards because they refused to use the Book of Common Prayer. The cemetery, shaded by large plane trees, is home to a number of monuments to well-known writers – Daniel Defoe, John Bunyan and William Blake among others – and also the last resting place of some members of Cromwell's family.

Wesley's Chapel
Opening times: 10am–4pm Mon–Sat (closed for services 12.45–1.30pm Thur)
Admission free (donations welcome)
www.wesleychapel.org.uk
Tel: 020-7253 2262

Bunhill Fields
Opening times: 8am–7pm (or dusk) Mon–Fri; 7.30am–7pm (or dusk)
Sat and Sun
Admission free

Did You Know?
John Milton wrote *Paradise Lost* while living in Bunhill Row, at the western edge of the cemetery.

Whitbread's Brewery 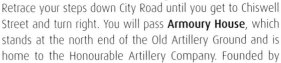 ⑩

Retrace your steps down City Road until you get to Chiswell Street and turn right. You will pass **Armoury House**, which stands at the north end of the Old Artillery Ground and is home to the Honourable Artillery Company. Founded by Henry VIII in 1537, the Company used to be housed in the priory which gave Spitalfields its name: St Mary Spital. It moved to its current site in 1658. This attractive and striking building replaces a smaller 17th-century armoury, the central portion of which was completed in 1735 to designs by Thomas Stibbs. Its distinctive flag tower was added in 1802, and the east and west wings were built in 1828. A cottage, originally for the Sergeant Major, was built against the west wing in 1850. The Honourable Artillery Company plays a ceremonial role in providing guards of honour during state visits paid to the City of London.

Across the road is **Whitbread's Brewery**. In 1736, 16-year-old Samuel Whitbread became apprenticed to a brewer in Bedford; when he died, 60 years later, his Chiswell Street brewery was producing nearly a million litres (200,000 gallons) a year. Whitbread bought the building in 1750 and it was used as a brewery until 1976. It is now hired for private functions and is no longer open to the public. The Porter Tun Room, now a banqueting suite, has the largest timber-post roof in Europe, with a span of 18 metres (60 feet).

Whitbread's Brewery
www.thebrewery.co.uk
Tel: 020-7638 8811

Barbican ⑪

Continue along Chiswell Street and turn left onto Silk Street and you will see the Barbican complex ahead of you. A 'barbican' is a defensive gate or tower – a reference to the old Roman walls of London that can still be seen nearby. The excuse for this riot of concrete and grimy glass was a particularly bad night of bombing in December 1940, which flattened the entire area. Eventually redeveloped in the 1960s, it was an ambitious plan by London County Council, who asked architects Chamberlin, Powell and Bon to provide as much open space and as many dwelling units as possible. The architects built a large part of the scheme on a series of interlinked podia, which actually manages to impart a pleasantly spacious feel in spite of the high density of housing (and all the concrete). It is still a confusing place, though, unless you know it well; the many signposts and yellow lines on the pavement do little to mitigate this difficulty.

Apart from the residential tower blocks, there is an arts complex with a concert hall, two theatres, two cinemas, two galleries, and an excellent library with special sections for children and music, as well as an unexpectedly lovely conservatory. The complex also includes canals, an ornamental lake and fountains. Sections of London's old city wall are to be found at the south-west corner (near the Museum of London). The Guildhall School of Music and Drama is also located within the Barbican.

Sitting at the heart of the complex, and looking, frankly, a little lost, is **St Giles**, **Cripplegate**, a church built in 1550 that survived the Great Fire of London only to be so badly damaged by World War II bombing that only its tower was left standing. It was rebuilt in the 1950s and now acts as the parish church for the Barbican. The poet John Milton was buried here in 1674.

Barbican Centre
Opening times: 9am–11pm Mon–Sat; 11am–11pm Sun; noon–11pm public holidays; admission free
www.barbican.org.uk
Tel: 020-7638 8891 (box office)

St Giles, Cripplegate
Opening times: 10am–4pm Mon–Fri
Admission free
www.stgilescripplegate.co.uk

St Giles, Cripplegate, Barbican

Museum of London ⑫

Located to the southwest of the Barbican, at the junction of London Wall and Aldersgate Street, the Museum of London opened in 1976 and provides a lively account of London life from prehistoric times to the present day. The city's history is told vividly through a series of reconstructed interiors and street scenes, and displays of domestic artefacts and archaeological findings. Some of the best exhibits are on Roman and medieval London, and there is a special display on the Great Fire of 1666 called 'London's Burning'. There are plans to move the museum to a new site near Smithfield Market by 2021.

Museum of London
Opening times: 10am–6pm daily; admission free
www.museumoflondon.org.uk
Tel: 020-7001 9844

St Botolph's, Aldersgate ⑬

Across the junction of London Wall and Aldersgate Street stands St Botolph's, Aldersgate (on the corner of the street called Little Britain). This modest late-Georgian church is one of three dedicated to St Botolph in the City – the other two are at Aldgate and Bishopsgate. This elegant gem replaces a 14th-century place of worship and its staid exterior conceals a surprisingly flamboyant and well-preserved interior. There is a finely decorated plaster ceiling, a

magnificent organ and lovely galleries. Unusually, the box pews were kept in the galleries rather than in the main body of the church. There is also a fine oak pulpit resting somewhat incongruously on a carving of a palm tree. The original churchyard was converted into a park in 1880, which came to be known as Postman's Park, as it was where workers from the nearby Post Office headquarters took their breaks. Victorian painter and sculptor G.F. Watts dedicated one of the church's walls to a collection of commemorative plaques honouring acts of bravery by ordinary people in the late 19th century; some of these can still be seen.

St Botolph's, Aldersgate
Services: Noon–3pm Thur; admission free
Tel: 020-7606 0684

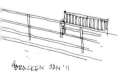

BRACKEN JAN '11

Archway leading to St Bartholomew-the-Great

St Bartholomew-the-Great ⑭

Walk along Little Britain, crossing the junction with King Edward Street and Montague Street, until you come to the open space at West Smithfield. You will see a narrow three-storey half-timbered Tudor building over a stone archway on your right. Pass under, and the church of St Bartholomew-the-Great is at the end of the walkway.

This is one of the best preserved medieval church interiors in London. It is also thought to be London's old parish church, founded in 1123 by a monk called Rahere – a courtier to Henry I – who dreamt that St Bartholomew had saved him from a winged monster. The archway was the original entrance to the church in the 13th century, before the nave was pulled down when Henry

VIII dissolved the monasteries. The present church building of St Bartholomew-the-Great retains its original crossing and chancel, and its round arches have some fine Norman detailing. There are also some good Tudor monuments. The church is popular with film-makers seeking an authentic Tudor interior. It really is a gem.

Today this medieval archway overlooks West Smithfield – which used to be the church's burial grounds – and **St Bartholomew's Hospital**, which has stood on this site since 1123. Some of its existing buildings date from 1759. **Cloth Fair**, the small street that runs alongside St Bartholomew-the-Great, has two houses – Nos. 41 and 42 – that survived the Great Fire of London in 1666, although they have in the intervening years been modernised. The name comes from the Bartholomew Fair – the main cloth fair in medieval England, held annually at Smithfield until it was suppressed in 1855, due to the Victorians' revulsion at the fair's reputation for debauchery. Cloth Fair was also home to the poet laureate John Betjeman, who lived at No. 43 for most of his life. It is now possible to stay in the house, which has been turned into guest accommodation, to experience the flavour of this part of the city.

St Bartholomew-the-Great
Opening times: 8.30am–5pm (4pm in winter) Mon–Fri; 10.30am–4pm Sat; 8.30am–8pm Sun; 10.20am–8pm bank holidays
Admission free
www.greatstbarts.com

> **Did You Know?**
> Benjamin Franklin worked for a printer based in the Lady Chapel of St Bartholomew-the-Great in 1725.

Charterhouse ⑮

Leave Cloth Fair and cross Long Lane onto Hayne Street, at the top of which you will see Charterhouse Square. It is almost as if a little bit of Oxford or some English country town has been magically transported to this part of the city. The Tudor gateway on the north side of this charming, irregularly shaped cobblestone square leads into a former Carthusian monastery, which was dissolved by Henry VIII, and in 1611 turned into a hospital. Intended for poor pensioners, it also housed a charity school, called Charterhouse. John Wesley studied there, as did the writer William Thackeray and Robert Baden-Powell, founder of the Boy Scouts movement. The school moved out to Godalming in Surrey in 1872, and is now an exclusive boarding school. Part of the original monastery site was then taken over by the medical school of St Bartholomew's Hospital and has recently been converted into a museum, under the aegis of the Museum of London. Some of the original buildings have survived, including the chapel and part of its cloisters. It is possible to visit this historic site on a pre-booked tour. It is also available for hire for private functions, and the public are welcome to attend services in the chapel.

Charterhouse
Visits can only be made as part of a pre-booked tour or to attend
chapel services
Admission charges
www.thecharterhouse.org

Smithfield Market ⑯

This vast market building, officially designated Central London Markets but more commonly known as Smithfield Market, runs down the south side of Charterhouse Street. Tall, octagonal cupolas dominate the corners of the long red-brick–and-stone building. Designed by Horace Jones, it was completed in 1867; some useful additions were made in the 20th century, such as the glass roofs which project from the sides of the building (which however obscure the stone carving of the arches).

Animals have been traded at Smithfield since the 12th century – a time when the area was well outside the city walls – and it has also acted as London's main public execution place. The site was granted its first official charter in 1400 and officially established as a cattle market in 1648; live cattle continued to be sold here until the middle of the 19th century.

Now it confines itself to wholesale meat and poultry, and is widely regarded as one of the best equipped meat markets in the world. Some neighbouring pubs keep market hours, serving hearty breakfasts from dawn. The best time to see the market in full swing is around 7am; by mid-morning, business is pretty much completed.

Smithfield Market
Opening times: 2am–noon Mon–Fri
Admission free
www.smithfieldmarket.com

Link to the City walk: Cross West Smithfield and walk down Giltspur Street until you come to Old Bailey.

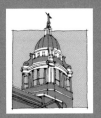

The City

Nearest Tube: St Paul's
Approximate walking time: 2 hours 30 minutes

The City

The City of London is one of the world's most important financial districts, home to such venerable institutions as the Bank of England and the Stock Exchange. Originally a Roman settlement, it flourished as an urban centre right through the Middle Ages and Renaissance. Most traces of these earlier incarnations were obliterated, however, by the Great Fire of 1666, and then the aerial bombardment of World War II. Architecturally the area is a magnificent mix of styles, everything from late 17th-century churches (many by Wren), through the 18th and 19th centuries' elegant Neoclassical temples (dedicated to commerce rather than religion), right up to the skyscrapers of the present day. It is this melange of old and new, squat and tall, stone and brick and glass that gives the district its distinctive character – its *genius loci*.

THE CITY

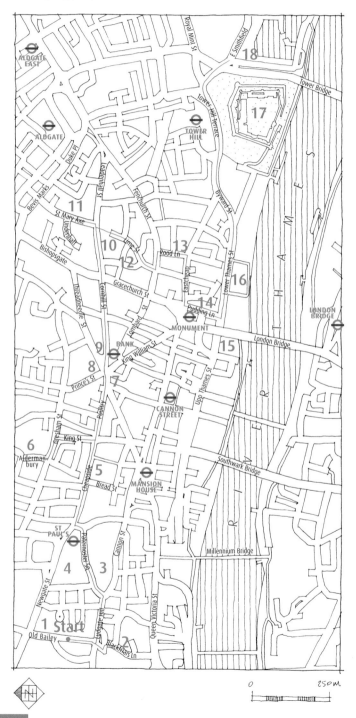

ALDGATE
EAST

ALDGATE

Bevis Marks

Duke Pl

11

St Mary Axe

Undershaft

10

Bishopsgate

Lime St

12

Threadneedle St

Gracechurch St

Cornhill St

BANK

9

8

King William St

Prince's St

7

Poultry

CANNON
STREET

6

Gresham St

King St

Alder-
bury

5

Cheapside

Bread St

MANSION
HOUSE

ST
PAUL'S

4

3

Newgate St

Old Bailey

1 Start

Ludgate Hill

Blackfriars Ln

2

Cannon St

Queen Victoria St

Royal Mint St

E Smithfield

18

Tower Bridge

17

Tower Hill Terrace

TOWER
HILL

Byward St

Tower Thames St

13

Rood Ln

Eastcheap

16

14

Pudding Ln

MONUMENT

London Bridge

15

LONDON
BRIDGE

London Bridge

Upp Thames St

Southwark Bridge

Millennium Bridge

T H A M E S

R

0   250 M

32

KEY

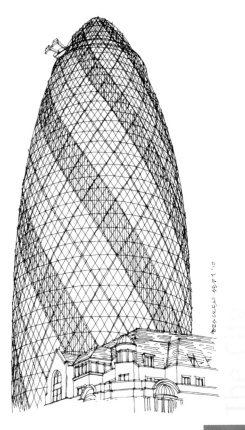

1. Old Bailey
2. Apothecaries' Hall
3. St Paul's Cathedral
4. Stock Exchange
5. St Mary-le-Bow
6. Guildhall Art Gallery
7. Mansion House
8. Bank of England Museum
9. Royal Exchange
10. Lloyd's of London
11. 30 St Mary Axe
12. Leadenhall Market
13. St Margaret Pattens
14. Monument
15. Fishmongers' Hall
16. Old Billingsgate
17. Tower of London
18. St Katherine's Dock

Old Bailey

Old Bailey ❶

Leave St Paul's station and walk along Newgate Street until you come to the Old Bailey on your left. The prominent dome, topped by a statue of Justice, is a paragon of Edwardian elegance.

The new Central Criminal Courts opened here in 1907, on the site of the notorious Newgate Prison. Public hangings used to take place outside the prison gates; these were stopped in 1868, but the Magpie and Stump pub across the road would serve a special 'execution breakfast' for those who had worked up a healthy appetite watching the spectacle. Judges still carry small posies of flowers into court with them on special days – a reminder of the times when the smell of those on trial was too much for their well-bred nostrils. Today, the courts are distinctly less pungent, and open to the public via a guided tour which starts in the Viaduct pub on Newgate Street and includes a visit to one of Newgate Prison's original cells – in what is now the

pub's cellar. It is possible to then visit one of the Old Bailey's courtrooms and watch a case in progress (this is in fact the only way to do such a thing any more because strict security precautions mean the public can no longer wander around the building).

Old Bailey
Access by guided tour only; admission charges
www.old-bailey.com/visiting-the-old-bailey
Tel: 07866 690618

Apothecaries' Hall ❷

Continue down Old Bailey, crossing Ludgate Hill onto Blackfriars Lane and you will come to the small but ornate entrance to the Apothecaries' Hall on your left. London's livery companies, also known as guilds, were established from the early Middle Ages onwards to protect and regulate specific trades.

The Worshipful Society of Apothecaries of London was founded in 1617 when it broke away from the older Grocers' Company. It went on to found the Chelsea Physic Garden in 1673, which has one of the richest collections of medicinal plants in Europe. The society's membership consisted of those who prepared, prescribed or sold drugs. Now nearly all members are either physicians or surgeons. It has produced some surprising alumni, including Oliver Cromwell and John Keats.

Apothecaries' Hall, originally called Cobham House, was destroyed in the Great Fire; a new hall was built in 1672, based on a design by Edward Jerman. Major restoration work was carried out in the 1780s, and even though the hall underwent further redevelopment in the 1980s, it still retains its 18th-century character. It is the oldest surviving livery company hall in the City of London.

Apothecaries' Hall

Apothecaries' Hall
Opening times (courtyard):
10am–5pm Mon–Fri
Admission free
www.apothecaries.org

St Paul's Cathedral ❸

Retrace your steps to Ludgate Hill and you will see St Paul's Cathedral on your right. Dominating the city skyline, Sir Christopher Wren's masterpiece has been the magnificent backdrop for such important state occasions as the funeral of Winston Churchill in 1965 and the marriage of Prince Charles to Lady Diana Spencer in 1981.

St Paul's Cathedral

BRACKEN JAN '11

Wren had submitted designs for the renovation of the old St Paul's before the Great Fire of London destroyed it in 1666. He was then asked to design a new building, which he did in 1673. Called the Great Model (which can be seen in the cathedral), it was rejected because it was in the form of a Greek cross, whereas the clergy preferred a Latin cross, which would allow them a larger nave for special occasions. Wren then produced what is known as the Warrant Design, which was accepted this time, and constructed between 1675 and 1710.

Visitors to St Paul's are invariably struck by the cool, spacious, beautifully ordered interior. The climax of Wren's design is doubtless the crossing, with its great dome, which at 110 metres (360 feet) high, is the second tallest in the world (after St Peter's, in the Vatican). The outer and inner layers actually hide a third structure, which supports the massive stone lantern on top – a unique solution to a daunting engineering problem. The southern tower contains the stunning geometrical staircase, a spiral of 92 stone steps leading to the cathedral library. Another staircase, from the south aisle, leads to the Whispering Gallery, whose strange acoustics enable the softest utterances to echo around the dome. Famous tombs in the cathedral include Wren's own – complete with the famous inscription, 'Reader, if you seek my monument, look around you' – as well as those of Florence Nightingale and the poet John Donne, whose monument was the only one to survive the Great Fire.

St Paul's Cathedral
Cathedral: 8.30am–4.30pm Mon–Sat
Dome galleries: 9.30am–4.15pm Mon–Sat
www.stpauls.co.uk

Did You Know?
Inigo Jones built a portico for the original cathedral's west front in 1634–40, which was in its time the largest one north of the Alps. It burnt down, along with the rest of the cathedral, in the Great Fire.

Note on Sir Christopher Wren (1632–1723)
One of England's most acclaimed architects, Wren was responsible for the rebuilding of more than 50 churches in the City of London after the Great Fire of 1666, including his masterpiece, St Paul's Cathedral.

Born into a well-placed establishment family – his father was Dean of Windsor and an uncle was Bishop of Ely – Wren began his career as an astronomer, geometer and mathematician-physicist, and only became interested in architecture around 1660. He held the Savilian Chair of Astronomy at Oxford from 1661 to 1673 and was a founder of the Royal Society (and its president 1680–82); his scientific work was highly regarded by the likes of Isaac Newton and Blaise Pascal. As befitted his family connections, most of Wren's commissions came from the church and the state.

To Wren, the Great Fire in 1666 would have seemed a heaven-sent opportunity to redesign the overcrowded medieval city along grandiose Neoclassical lines (something he had admired when visiting Paris – his one and only trip abroad). His famous reconstruction plan consisted of wide boulevards radiating from numerous piazzas in straight lines – anticipating Baron Haussmann's Paris by two centuries – but it was considered too radical for its time. The plan did, however, get him the job of Surveyor General of the King's Works in 1669. The parliamentary act for the rebuilding of the city was passed in 1670, and Wren spent the next 16 years designing 52 new churches.

Since there had been little church-building in England since the Reformation, no one had given any thought to what an Anglican church ought to look like. Wren went back to basics, setting down the practical guidelines that no church should be too large for the congregation to see or hear what was going on. Another massive challenge was the irregularity of the medieval sites that these new churches had to be built on. Much ingenuity was needed to fit these handsome Neoclassical buildings onto them, yet he managed to do so with an elegance, energy and breadth of design that is still delightful today.

Did You Know?

Even though Wren's steeples are often the most arresting features of his churches, these were often only designed and added as much as 20 years later. The steeple is in fact a typically Gothic feature, and until Wren added them, they were unheard of on Neoclassical buildings. His genius in successfully melding Gothic forms with Neoclassical style influenced church design for centuries.

Stock Exchange ❹

Located just to the north of St Paul's, overlooking Paternoster Square, is London's Stock Exchange. London wasn't just the capital of the British Empire, it was also the world's financial capital from the 18th to the 20th century. The city's first stock exchange was established in Threadneedle Street by a group of stockbrokers in 1801. Previously they used to meet in coffee houses. Although eclipsed by New York and Tokyo for several decades in the mid-1900s, London's importance as an international financial centre was boosted in 1986 by the 'Big Bang' – the deregulation of its financial markets.

The building's foyer contains a remarkable kinetic sculpture, *The Source*, which indicates the day's market performance through a three-dimensional matrix of mobile spheres.

St Mary-le-Bow ❺

Leave Paternoster Square via Cheapside and, past Bread Street, St Mary-le-Bow will be on your right. This church was founded here around 1080 as the London headquarters of the Archbishops of Canterbury. Rebuilt by Wren after

St Mary-le-Bow

it was destroyed in the Great Fire, it takes its name from the bow arches in its crypt, which date back to the Norman period. Wren echoed this motif in the graceful arches of his steeple, at the summit of which is an amazing weathervane in the form of a dragon. The church was bombed during the Blitz, leaving only the steeple and two outer walls standing, but was restored between 1956 and 1962. Its famous bells were recast and rehung.

St Mary-le-Bow
Opening times: 7.30am–6pm Mon–Wed, 7.30am–6.30pm Thur, 7.30am–4pm Fri
Admission free
www.stmarylebow.co.uk

Guildhall Art Gallery ❻

Continue along Cheapside, turn left onto King Street, then left again onto Gresham Street. Take the first right and the Guildhall will be on your right overlooking Aldermanbury Square.

Built around 1440, the **Guildhall** has been the administrative centre of the City of London for more than eight centuries. Its main hall, which gives the whole building its name, was for a long time used for trials, where judges condemned many people to death, including Henry Garnet, one of the Gunpowder plotters. Today, it is used for happier occasions, such as the banquet that takes place a few days after the Lord Mayor's Parade, and where the prime minister is always the keynote speaker. The interior is not open to the public.

Next door, the **Guildhall Art Gallery** houses the Corporation of London's art collection. It contains portraits from the 16th century up to the present day, and is also home to the studio collection of 20th-century artist Sir Matthew Smith. The current building is a replica of the 1885 original, which was destroyed by World War II bombing. In 1988, the remains of a Roman amphitheatre were discovered beneath the gallery. Dating back to 70 CE, it would have been capable of holding up to 6000 spectators in its time. Access to the ruins is included with the gallery admission.

Guildhall Art Gallery
Opening times: 10am–5pm Mon–Sat; noon–4pm Sun; admission charges
www.guildhall.cityoflondon.gov.uk/art-gallery

Mansion House ❼　

Retrace your steps to Cheapside and turn left onto Poultry; you will see the Mansion House ahead of you.

Overlooking this busy junction is **No. 1 Poultry**, a swaggering Post-modernist building decorated in bands of pastel-coloured stone (you can see an illustration of it in the Architectural Styles chapter). Located as it is on a tight corner, and rubbing shoulders with some of the City's most majestic buildings, it pretty much had to shout to make its presence felt. Architect James Stirling's genius was to create a building with presence, style and wit in this hemmed-in space. Its most remarkable feature is the ship-like prow overlooking the junction, which contains a restaurant, a roof garden, and an observation deck over the clock tower.

The **Mansion House** is the official home of the Lord Mayor of the City of London. It was completed in 1753 to a Palladian design by George Dance the Elder, and its main façade, with Corinthian columns, is a famous City landmark. The state rooms are magnificent, particularly the 27-metre (90-foot) Egyptian Hall. Less magnificent, but a reminder of the Lord Mayor's role as Chief Magistrate of the City, were the 11 holding cells (these have now been moved to the Museum of London).

Located behind the Mansion House is the Lord Mayor's parish church, **St Stephen Walbrook**. Built by Christopher Wren in 1672–79 (the spire added in 1717), it ranks among his finest work. The church's dome – unusual, though attractive – was clearly an experiment for St Paul's. It sits atop a brilliant, spatially daring combination of aisled nave and centralised plan, and floats gracefully on eight slender columns instead of the massive piers usually encountered. The church contains some lovely carvings, in stark contrast to which is the simplicity of Henry Moore's massive stone altar, added in 1987. There is also a moving tribute to Rector Chad Varah, founder of the Samaritans: a telephone in a glass box.

Mansion House
Tours: 2pm Tue; admission charges
www.cityoflondon.gov.uk

St Stephen Walbrook
Opening times: 10am–4pm Mon, Tue, Thur; 11am–3pm Wed, 10am–3.30pm Fri
Admission free
www.ststephenwalbrook.net

Did You Know?
Emmaline Pankhurst, the suffragette, was held for a time in the Mansion House cells.

Bank of England Museum ❽

Facing the Mansion House is the hefty bulk of the Bank of England – a suitably solid edifice for an institution with so weighty a function. In fact this is a dull, over-decorated behemoth that all but ignores its prime city location, preferring to turn a windowless face to the street and focus secretively inwards.

The Bank of England was originally set up in 1694 to raise money for the country's wars, and gradually developed into a national central bank with the power to issue banknotes. The 1788 building was originally designed by Sir John Soane, but only its exterior survives; the rest was destroyed in the 1920s and '30s when the bank was enlarged. Soane's stock office (from 1793) has since been reconstructed.

The building contains a museum that outlines the history of England's national finances, as well as displays of gold ingots, silver-plated decorations and a Roman mosaic floor, which were discovered during rebuilding.

Bank of England Museum
Opening times: 10am–5pm Mon–Fri; admission free
www.bankofengland.co.uk/museum
Tel: 020-7601 5545

Royal Exchange ⑨

Between the Bank of England and the Mansion House lies the Royal Exchange. This imposing Neoclassical building, dating from 1844, is the third to occupy the site since Sir Thomas Gresham founded the institution in 1565. Designed by Sir William Tite, it follows the original building's plan of a four-sided structure surrounding a central courtyard where merchants could do business – this

Royal Exchange

plan based on a bourse that Gresham had seen in Antwerp. The interior, designed by Edward I'Anson, is notable for its early use of concrete. The pediment contains a sculpture by Richard Westmacott (the younger). The Royal Exchange has been the beating heart of London's commerce since Elizabeth I gave it its royal charter, and it is still used as one

The City

of the sites from which the announcement of a new monarch is made. This tradition of commerce has recently been continued with the opening of the Royal Exchange as a luxury shopping and dining outlet. The equestrian statue in the forecourt is of the Duke of Wellington. There is also a war memorial dedicated to London troops closer to the front of the Exchange.

St Mary Woolnoth, which can be seen on the corner of Lombard Street and King William Street, is a striking work by Nicholas Hawksmoor (a pupil of Wren's). Lombard Street takes its name from the Italian bankers who settled here in the 13th century.

Royal Exchange
Opening times: 7am–11pm daily (shops and restaurants vary); admission free
www.theroyalexchange.co.uk

St Mary Woolnoth
Opening times: 9.30am–4.30pm Mon–Fri; admission free
www.london-city-churches.org.uk/Churches/StMaryWoolnoth/index.html
Tel: 020-7626 9701

Lloyd's of London ⑩

Walk along Cornhill Street, which turns into Leadenhall Street, and you will see Lloyd's of London towering over you. This is one of the gems of London's architecture, a visionary masterpiece of late 20th-century design.

Named after Edward Lloyd, the owner of a coffee shop where the business of insurance was invented in 1688, Lloyd's is one of the world's most famous insurance companies. When they decided they needed a new building in 1986, they turned to Richard Rogers, who had made his name with the Pompidou Centre in Paris. This building continues in the High Tech mode that Rogers pioneered with Renzo Piano in Paris, with its ducts and cranes, pods, pipes and braces, external glass lifts (the first of their kind in the country) and soaring staircase towers finished in shiny metal. The decision to express the building's services on the outside was a highly controversial one, but it was done in order to leave the interior spaces as uncluttered as possible.

The magnificent Underwriting Room soars a breathtaking 60 metres (200 feet), forming an airy atrium lit by daylight through its barrel-vaulted glass roof. Known somewhat ominously as 'The Room', it contains the famous Lutine Bell, which is rung in the event of a disaster. The building's 11th floor houses the Committee Room, which is where a dining room (designed originally for the Earl of Shelburne in 1763 by Robert Adam) was moved piece by piece from its previous location in Lloyd's 1958 building across the road.

Directly opposite Lloyd's on Leadenhall Street (at No. 122) stands the Leadenhall Building, one of a number of recently built skyscrapers that have been given a colourful nickname due to an unusual shape – in this case a wedge, hence the name **'The Cheesegrater'**. Designed by Rogers Stirk

Harbour and Partners, it opened in 2014 and is the second tallest building in the City of London (at 225 metres or 738 feet). The tallest, Heron Tower, at 110 Bishopsgate, is actually only 202 metres (663 feet) at roof height but has a 28-metre (92 foot) mast.

30 St Mary Axe ⓫

Diagonally across Leadenhall Street from The Cheesegrater, on the corner of Lime Street, stands another skyscraper with a colourful nickname: **'The Scalpel'**. This elegant 38-storey edifice was designed by Kohn Pedersen Fox for the insurance company W.R. Berkley. Completed in 2018, it is their new European headquarters and they occupy about a quarter of the total floor area. There is some commercial space at ground level as well as a basement restaurant accessed via Leadenhall Street. The *Financial Times* gave the building its nickname because of its sharply articulated angular facades.

Walk up St Mary Axe and you will pass the church of **St Andrew Undershaft** on your right. It is a lightly handled Gothic church with a medieval-looking tower all executed in a pale-yellow stone.

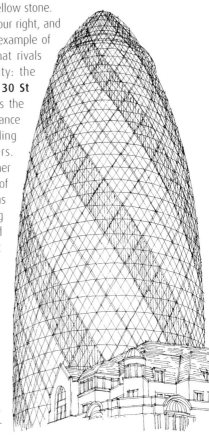

Farther along the street, also on your right, and towering over the church, is another example of London's architectural daring, one that rivals Lloyd's of London for sheer audacity: the 40-storey 'Gherkin'. Officially called **30 St Mary Axe**, it was originally known as the Swiss Re Tower, after the Swiss reinsurance group who commissioned the building from architects Foster and Partners. Resembling a giant cigar – a not altogether inappropriate image for the fat cats of the City – and with its swirling patterns of diamond-shaped glass, the building was an instant hit when completed and soon became one of London's most recognisable landmarks. The building's double-layered skin creates a natural chimney effect that reduces the need for air-conditioning. The design also allows for maximum natural lighting. At the top of the tower, just beneath its conical glass dome, is a stunning, double-height rooftop gallery and restaurant for tenants and their guests.

Across St Mary Axe, on Undershaft, sits **St Helen's Bishopsgate**, an odd-looking 13th-century church which houses the tomb of Sir Thomas Gresham, the founder of the Royal Exchange. Its strange shape owes to the fact that it was originally two places of worship: a parish church and the chapel of a nunnery. The nuns of St Helen's were notorious for a bizarre form of worship known as 'secular kissing'.

St Andrew Undershaft
Open by appointment only; admission free
www.london-city-churches.org.uk/Churches/StAndrewUndershaft/index.html
Tel: 020-7283 2231

St Helen's Bishopsgate
Opening times: 9.30am–5pm Mon–Fri; admission free
www.st-helens.org.uk
Tel: 020-7283 2231

Leadenhall Market

Leadenhall Market

Retrace your steps to Leadenhall Street, cross it and go down Lime street until you come to Leadenhall Place on your right and you will see one of the entrances to Leadenhall Market in front of you.

This elaborate and ornately decorated covered mall was designed by Sir Horace Jones in 1881 (Jones also designed the nearby Billingsgate Fish Market). This food market is very popular at lunchtime with City workers. Its sells traditional game, poultry, fish and meat and also has a number of independent shops offering everything from wine to chocolates to cheese. Its name derives from a 14th-century mansion that used to stand here, which had a lead roof. There has been a food market here since the Middle Ages, and in Roman times this was the site of the forum. One of the most delightful little streets in London – to walk under its ornate roof is like entering a secret Dickensian world.

Leadenhall Market
Opening times: 24 hours daily (shops and restaurants vary)
www.leadenhallmarket.co.uk

St Margaret Pattens

Browse Leadenhall Market at your leisure, then exit onto Leadenhall Place and turn right onto Lime Street. Walk to the end and take a left onto Fenchurch Street and you will see **'The Walkie-Talkie'** across the street at Nos. 18–20. Completed in 2014, this 38-storey building by Rafael Viñoly has a distinctive top-heavy shape, spreading outwards as it climbs. This was done to maximise floor space at the top of the building, where rent is usually higher, but resulted in a somewhat inelegant shape, earning it the Carbuncle Cup, an unofficial award for bad architecture. Originally planned to be 200 metres (656 feet) tall, concerns about its visual impact on nearby St Paul's Cathedral and the Tower of London kept its height to 160 metres (525 feet). The **Sky Garden** on the top three storeys, billed as the city's highest public garden, contains a large viewing deck, a bar and restaurants.

Turn right onto Rood Lane and St Margaret Pattens will be on your left at the corner of Eastcheap. This is another of Wren's post-fire churches. Built between 1684 and 1687, it was named after a type of overshoe that used to be made nearby. The church's rather plain-looking spire dominates this narrow, hilly corner. At 60 metres (200 feet) this is Wren's third highest and was the only one he designed in a medieval style; hence it is sometimes referred to as his only 'true spire', even as it is not one of his best efforts. It is one of only a handful of City churches that escaped significant damage during World War II.

The interior is simple and contains the only canopied pews in London. The initials 'C.W.' which appear on one of the pews are sometimes thought to refer to Christopher Wren, but more likely refer to the church wardens who sat here. Look out, too, for the punishment box, where wrongdoers had to sit during the service. This is carved with a devil's head.

In 1954 St Margaret Pattens ceased to be a parish church, becoming one of the City's guild churches instead. It holds regular services on weekdays, rather than on Sundays – to cater to office workers.

Sky Garden
Opening times: 9.30am–5.30pm Mon–Fri
Admission free
www.skygarden.london/sky-garden
Tel: 020-7337 2344

St Margaret Pattens
Opening times: 10.30am–4pm Mon–Fri
Admission free
www.stmargaretpattens.org
Tel: 020-7623 6630

Monument ⑭

Turn right onto Eastcheap from Rood Lane and Monument will be on your left on Pudding Lane. This towering structure, designed by Sir Christopher Wren to commemorate the Great Fire of London, is the tallest freestanding stone column in the world. Its height of 62 metres (205 feet) marks its distance – 62 metres – from where the fire started, in Pudding Lane. This was on 2 September 1666, in a baker's shop owned by Thomas Farriner, the king's baker. His maid had failed to put out the ovens at the end of the night's work and the heat caused the old wooden building to ignite – the maid was one of the fire's victims. Once started, it spread quickly – the city was built primarily of wood and the summer had been very dry. Strong winds fanned the flames. The fire destroyed 84 churches, as well as the old St Paul's Cathedral. It also burned away vast areas of slums that had been infested with plague the previous year – thus in a way giving the city a fresh start.

Reliefs around the column's base show Charles II restoring the city. Three hundred and eleven steps lead to a viewing platform; the views are magnificent.

Monument
Opening times: 9.30am–6pm (Apr–Sep), 9.30am–5.30pm (Oct–Mar)
Admission charges
www.themonument.info

Fishmongers' Hall ⑮

On the other side of London Bridge from Monument sits Fishmongers' Hall, a startlingly beautiful Neoclassical building overlooking the river. Consisting of

Monument

six Ionic engaged columns rising two storeys over a rusticated arched base to support a pediment, it was built in 1834 to a design by Henry Roberts (although his assistant George Gilbert Scott made the drawings), and after being badly damaged by bombing in December 1940, restored by Austen Hall and reopened in 1951.

Back on the Monument side of London Bridge stands the church of **St Magnus the Martyr**. St Magnus was the Earl of the Orkney Islands and a renowned Norwegian Christian leader; he was brutally murdered in 1110. There has been a church here for over 1000 years. When Christopher Wren built the replacement for the one that burnt down in the Great Fire between 1671 and 1676, it was at the foot of London Bridge, which until 1738 was the only bridge across the Thames. Wren's magnificent arched porch spanned the flagstones leading to the old bridge, which meant that everyone going south from the city had to pass underneath it. (Sadly, this route is no longer available.) The interior contains a delicately carved organ case depicting musical instruments, and Wren's pulpit, which was restored in 1924.

Fishmongers' Hall
Guided tours by appointment
Admission charges
www.fishhall.co.uk
Tel: 020-7626 3531

St Magnus the Martyr
Opening times: 10am–4pm Tue–Fri; 10am–1.30pm Sun
Admission free
www.stmagnusthemartyr.org.uk
Tel: 020-7626 4481

Old Billingsgate ⑯

Continue along Lower Thames Street and you will come to Old Billingsgate on your right. This was for 900 years the location of London's main fish market. Sited on one of the city's earliest quays, it was one of London's noisiest markets and infamous for the foul language that rang through it. In the 19th and early 20th centuries, up to 400 tonnes of fish were sold here every day, much of it delivered by boat. The market moved to Canary Wharf in the Docklands in 1982.

The best views of the building are from the southern shore of the Thames, where the Neoclassicism of its design can best be appreciated. In fact, it looks more like a grand hotel than a fish market, with its arcaded base and elegantly proportioned windows. The restrained elegance of its design sits well over the water, where its reflection lends it an even more placid air of completeness – something the architect clearly considered. Sir Horace Jones designed the building in 1875 to replace the first Billingsgate Market, constructed in 1850 by John Jay. It is today a hospitality and events venue.

Across Lower Thames Street from Old Billingsgate is **St Mary-at-Hill**, one of Wren's first churches (1670–76). Its Greek-cross design was a prototype for his original – but unbuilt – plan for St Paul's Cathedral. The interior plasterwork and 17th-century furnishings both survived the Victorian era and its mania for 'refurbishment'. They even survived the bombs of World War II, only to be destroyed by fire in 1988. The building was then restored to its original appearance, only to be damaged again in 1992 – this time by an IRA bomb.

Continue along Lower Thames Street as it turns into the gently curving Byward Street and you will see **All Hallows by the Tower** on your right. The first church on this site was a Saxon one, while the arch on the southwest corner contains some Roman tiles. There are also some Roman pavement tiles in the crypt. Most of the church's interior has been altered, but a limewood font cover, carved by Grinling Gibbons in 1682, has survived. The church houses a small museum, a brass-rubbing centre and a bookstall. It also hosts occasional concerts. This is where Samuel Pepys watched the Great Fire of London, where William Penn, the founder of Pennsylvania Colony, was baptised, and where John Quincy Adams was married in 1797, before he became the sixth American president.

St Mary-at-Hill
Opening times: 10.15am–3.45pm Mon-Fri; admission free
www.stmary-at-hill.org
Tel: 020-7626 4184

All Hallows by the Tower
Opening times: 8am–6pm Mon–Fri, 10am–5pm Sat and Sun (Apr–Oct);
8am–5pm Mon–Fri, 10am–5pm Sat and Sun (Nov–Mar)
Admission free
www.allhallowsbythetower.org.uk
Tel: 020-7481 2928

Tower of London ⑰

Continue along Byward Street, which turns into Tower Hill, and you will see the great complex of the Tower of London on your right. The Tower of London is without a doubt London's most impressive and important tourist attraction, and has been drawing visitors since the days of Charles II (1660–85). This magnificent cluster of Norman towers was where the Crown Jewels and some of the armour of the royal collection were first displayed in public.

For much of its 900-year history, however, the Tower was a place of fear and misery, a prison where those accused of treason were incarcerated and tortured. Many never saw the light of day again. It was also a place of execution, although only aristocrats were executed here, on Tower Green, to spare them the indignity of the mobs of Tower Hill. In fact only seven people died here, two of them the unfortunate wives of Henry VIII. Aristocratic prisoners were held in Beauchamp Tower, often with retinues of their own servants to wait on them. The most mysterious and sinister deaths to have occurred in the Tower were the boy princes Edward and Richard, sons of Edward IV. Placed in the Tower by their uncle, Richard of Gloucester, when their father

died in 1483, neither of them was ever seen again. Richard crowned himself king later that year. In 1674 the skeletons of two children were found near what is known as the Bloody Tower.

The **White Tower** is the oldest surviving building in the complex – begun by William the Conqueror in 1077, and finished in 1097. At 30 metres (90 feet), it would have been the tallest building in London at the time. Built just inside the old Roman wall along the Thames, it contains an austerely beautiful Romanesque place of worship: the Chapel of St John. For centuries this particular tower served as the royal armoury; in the 1990s many of the exhibits were moved to other museums in Leeds and Portsmouth, but the most historic items have remained, including the Tudor and Stuart armour. Originally the tower's main rooms would have been at least twice their present height but extra floors were built in them in 1490.

The **Jewel House** is the home of the Crown Jewels, which are used at coronations and state occasions. Most of the Crown Jewels only date back to 1661, when a new set had to be made for the coronation of Charles II – parliament having destroyed the previous crowns and sceptres after the execution of Charles I in 1649. On display are ten crowns, three Swords of Justice (symbolising mercy, spiritual justice and temporal justice), the Orb – a

Tower of London

gold sphere encrusted with jewels – and the Sceptre, in which is set the world's largest cut diamond, the 530-carat Great Star of Africa.

Other buildings in the Tower include the **Medieval Palace**, built by Henry III in 1220 and enlarged by his son, Edward I, who also added **Traitors' Gate**, through which prisoners entered the Tower by boat. The **Queen's House** is the official residence of the Tower's governor, and the Yeoman Warders – more commonly known as the Beefeaters – also live in the Tower when guarding it.

Tower of London
Opening times: 9am–5.30pm Tue–Sat, 10am–5.30pm Sun–Mon (Mar–Oct); 9am–4.30pm Tue–Sat, 10am–4.30pm Sun–Mon (Nov–Feb)
Admission charges
www.hrp.org.uk/tower-of-london
Tel: 020-3166 6000

> **Did You Know?**
> Legend has it that if the ravens ever desert the Tower of London the kingdom will fall. (Taking no chances, obviously, the birds have part of their wings clipped on one side, making flight impossible.)

St Katherine's Dock ⑱

Across Tower Bridge Approach from the Tower of London is St Katherine's Dock. Originally the most centrally located of all London's docks, it was designed by Thomas Telford and opened in 1828. It handled everything from tea to live turtles – turtle soup being a popular Victorian delicacy. St Katherine's flourished until the middle of the 20th century, when containerisation meant that larger docks were needed; these were built farther downstream at Tilbury. The docks closed down in 1968, and languished until the 1980s, when they were redeveloped as residential, commercial and entertainment facilities. With the converted industrial buildings arranged around a network of waterways, walkways and bridges, St Katherine's Dock has come back to life – full of yachts and waterside cafes, and a wonderful place to stroll night or day.

St Katherine's Dock
www.skdocks.co.uk
Tel: 020-7264 5287

Link to Southwark walk: Cross Tower Bridge.

St Katherine's Dock

Southwark

Nearest Tube: Tower Hill
Approximate walking time: 1 hour 30 minutes

Southwark

Located on the south bank of the Thames, Southwark in Shakespeare's day fell outside the jurisdiction of the City of London; as a result it was possible here to get away with things that were banned in the City. Bear baiting and cock fighting were popular amusements, as were theatres – a far less genteel evening out than it is now. A replica of the Globe Theatre, where Shakespeare's company was based, has been built close to its original site. Borough High Street was lined with taverns and brothels, while The George is the last survivor of London's galleried inns. Southwark's reputation for raucous entertainment continued through the 18th and 19th centuries as the area became home to docks, warehouses and factories. Today the area has undergone considerable gentrification, with extensive renovation of existing buildings and the appearance of new cultural attractions such as the world-famous Tate Modern and the European Union's tallest skyscraper: The Shard.

SOUTHWARK

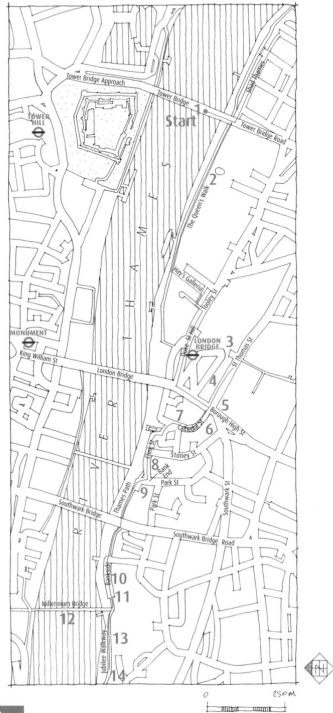

KEY

1. Tower Bridge
2. City Hall
3. The Shard
4. The Old Operating Theatre
5. George Inn
6. Borough Market
7. Southwark Cathedral
8. Clink Prison Museum
9. The Anchor
10. Shakespeare's Globe
11. Cardinal's Wharf
12. Millennium Bridge
13. Tate Modern
14. Bankside Gallery

Tower Bridge, Southwark and The Shard

Tower Bridge ❶

Leave Tower Hill station via Tower Hill and turn right onto Tower Bridge Approach. Completed in 1894, Tower Bridge immediately became a popular landmark. The Victorians were brilliant engineers; but they were afraid that too much innovation would look ugly. They tended to dress things up in antique-looking disguises, e.g. suspension bridges supported by Egyptian pylons. In this case, a remarkably clever engineering solution was tarted up to look like a cross between a cathedral and a castle. And yet, it has an uncannily balanced profile, and seems to manage to really pull it off. Certainly it has become one of the city's greatest icons.

The development of the East End of London in the 19th century meant that a new river crossing downstream from London Bridge was needed. The problem was that a traditional fixed bridge would prevent tall-masted ships from entering the Port of London facilities. A public competition in 1876 received over 50 designs and was eventually won by Sir Horace Jones. The engineer of the scheme, Sir John Wolfe Barry, came up with the idea of a combined bascule-and-suspension bridge: the central span made up of two equal parts (called bascules) could open to allow for river traffic, while the two side-spans were fixed suspension bridges. In its heyday it opened five times a day.

The bridge is home to the Tower Bridge Exhibition, which has interactive displays on the history of the bridge and includes a chance to see the steam engine that powered the lifting machinery until 1976 when the system was electrified.

Tower Bridge Exhibition
Opening times: 9.30am–5.30pm daily; admission charges
www.towerbridge.org.uk
Tel: 020-7403 3761

City Hall ❷

Left of Tower Bridge is **Shad Thames**, an atmospheric old area of Victorian docks and winding cobbled streets which was redeveloped in the 1980s into a popular residential area. Most of the warehouses have been converted into apartments, many with splendid views of the river. There are also plenty of bars and restaurants housed in the distinctive ground floors of these charming old buildings.

Retrace your steps up Shad Thames, past Tower Bridge, and you will come to the Queen's Walk. **City Hall** – looking like a hard-boiled egg that has been shelled and sliced, ready to go on a salad – will be in front of you. Designed by Norman Foster and opened in July 2002 to house the newly created Greater London Authority, the building has no front or rear in the conventional sense; its unusual, bulbous shape is intended to reduce surface area and improve its energy efficiency. A 500-metre (1,640 ft) helical walkway, reminiscent of Frank Lloyd Wright's Guggenheim Museum in New York, ascends the 10-storey building, providing views of the building's interior, intended to represent transparency – something Foster also made a feature in his design for the Reichstag in Berlin. At the top of the egg is an exhibition and meeting space called 'London's Living Room', which has an observation deck that is open to the public.

Farther along the Queen's Walk floats the World War II battleship **HMS Belfast**. Launched in 1938, this ship was instrumental in the destruction of the German battlecruiser *Scharnhorst* in the Battle of North Cape, and played an important role in the Normandy landings. After the war it was sent to work for the United Nations in Korea. It remained in service with the British navy until 1965. Since 1971 it has been a floating naval museum, part of which is a re-creation of what the ship would have been like in 1943. On weekends, children can take part in educational activities on board the ship.

London's Living Room
Opening times: 8am–5pm Mon–Fri; admission free
www.londonslivingroom.co.uk
Tel: 020-7983 4000

HMS Belfast
Opening times: 10am–6pm daily; admission charges
www.iwm.org.uk/visits/hms-belfast

> **Did You Know?**
> The original design for the City Hall proposed a giant sphere dangling over the Thames.

City Hall

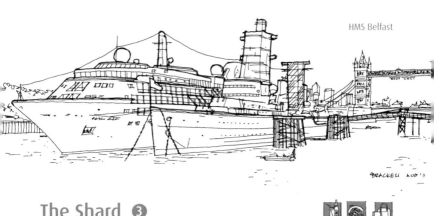

HMS Belfast

The Shard ❸

Continue along the Queen's Walk and turn left into the airy shopping centre known as **Hay's Galleria**. A curving street of 19th-century warehouses has been spectacularly roofed with a glass barrel-vault. Named after its original owner, the merchant Alexander Hay, who acquired a brewery here in 1651, the place was subsequently acquired by John Humphrey Jr in 1840 and converted into a wharf. Hay's Wharf became one of the country's chief delivery points for tea in the 19th century. Badly bombed in September 1940, the area fell into decline after the war. Redevelopment in 1987 saw the tea warehouses converted into offices and shops. The wharf was closed off and filled in, and the entire space roofed to create the galleria, one of the most delightful spaces in this part of the city.

Across Tooley Street sits the **London Dungeon**, an expanded version of the Chamber of Horrors at Madame Tussauds. Very popular with children, this fascinating museum highlights some of the most bloodthirsty events in British history, making clever use of live actors and special effects. The shows include the Great Plague, the Torture Chamber and Jack the Ripper.

Continue along Tooley Street as it turns into Duke Street Hill and you will see the massive form of **'The Shard'** towering above you. Designed by architect Renzo Piano, this 95-storey office and hotel complex takes the form of an irregularly shaped triangle and is entirely clad in glass. It was completed in 2012 and is 310 meters (985 feet) tall, making it the highest building not only in the United Kingdom but the European Union as well. There is a viewing gallery on the 72nd floor, with stunning views of the city and beyond.

London Dungeon
Tours: 10am–5pm daily; admission charges
www.thedungeons.com

The Shard
Opening times: 10am–10pm Thur–Sat; 10am–7pm Sun–Wed
Admission charges
www.the-shard.com

The Old Operating Theatre

Turn left from Duke Street Hill onto Borough High Street and then left onto St Thomas Street. The Old Operating Theatre will be on your left. This is the oldest operating theatre in the country, dating from 1822.

Guy's and St Thomas' Hospital was one of the oldest in Britain; it stood here from the 12th century until it was forced to move to Lambeth in 1862. Nearly all of its buildings were demolished to make way for a railway. The women's operating theatre (which is now the Old Operating Theatre Museum and Herb Garret) only survived because it happened to be located away from the hospital's main buildings, in a garret over the hospital church. It lay bricked up and forgotten until the 1950s. Now it has been fitted out like an operating theatre from the early 19th century – a grim time for anyone who needed surgery, since it was before the discovery of antiseptics or anaesthetic. The display shows how patients were gagged and blindfolded and then tied to the wooden operating table to stop them struggling when the surgeon's knife bit. A box of sawdust under the table caught the blood.

The Old Operating Theatre
Opening times: 2–5pm Mon; 10.30–5pm Tue–Sun; admission charges
www.oldoperatingtheatre.com
Tel: 020-7188 2679

George Inn

Return to Borough High Street and the George Inn will be at No. 77. This is the only surviving galleried inn in London. This old type of inn used to feature a first-floor gallery that led to the bedrooms and overlooked the main room, where guests would take their food and drink. It was rebuilt in 1676 after the fire which devastated Southwark, and its style dates back to the Middle Ages. Originally there would have been three wings around the courtyard, where plays would often have been staged, but only one wing remains today – the north and east wings having been demolished in 1889. The inn, now owned by the National Trust, is still a restaurant. During the summer, the yard is filled with picnic tables, and actors and Morris dancers attempt to amuse the patrons.

The **War Memorial** further down Borough High Street, erected in 1924, commemorates those who died in World War I.

George Inn
Opening times: 11am–11pm daily; admission free
Tel: 020-7407 2056

> **Did You Know?**
> Charles Dickens actually mentions the George Inn in *Little Dorrit*.

Borough Market ❻

Walk back up Borough High Street and Borough Market will be on your left. This is a popular market specialising in fine and gourmet food from all over Britain and Europe: quality fruit and vegetables, organic meats, fish and dairy produce. There has been a market on or near this site since 1276.

Located on the Southwark Street side of Borough Market is the **Hop Exchange**. With its easy access to Kent, where hops are grown, this part of London was ideal for the brewing of beer and trading of hops. The Hop Exchange building was constructed in 1866 to be the centre of that trade. Now converted into an office block, it retains its original pediment – complete with carvings depicting the hop harvest – and iron gates with a hop motif. It is unfortunately not open to the public.

Borough Market
Opening times: 10am–5pm Mon–Thur; 10am–6pm Fri; 8am–5pm Sat
(limited market on Mon and Tue); admission free
www.boroughmarket.org.uk

Southwark Cathedral ❼

Leave Borough Market and turn left up Cathedral Street. Southwark Cathedral will be on your right (you can see an illustration of it in the Architectural Styles chapter). Also known as the Cathedral and Collegiate Church of St Saviour and St Mary Overie, it is the main church for the Anglican Diocese of Southwark and has been a place of worship for more than a millennium. The present Gothic building is charming – though it looks a bit like it strayed in from a small country town to find itself crammed into this gritty urban setting. It dates from between 1220 and 1420, when it was part of a priory. The memorials are fascinating, including a late 13th-century wooden effigy of a knight, and a plaque commemorating Shakespeare's burial of his brother Edmund.

The cathedral was recently restored in a multi-million-pound restoration programme, which included the addition of new buildings, including a shop and a refectory. The grounds have been landscaped to create a herb garden as well as the attractive Millennium Courtyard that leads to the riverside.

Southwark Cathedral
Opening times: 9am–5pm Mon–Fri, 9.30am–3.45pm and 5–6pm Sat,
12.30–3pm and 4–6 pm Sun; admission free
www.cathedral.southwark.anglican.org
Tel: 020-7367 6700

Did You Know?
There is a chapel in Southwark Cathedral named in honour of a man called John Harvard, who was baptised here in 1607. He went on to found a rather famous university in America.

Clink Prison Museum ⑧

Return to Cathedral Street and follow it as it turns into Clink Street. You will see a replica of Sir Francis Drake's ship, the **Golden Hinde**, at Pickfords Wharf on your right. It was in the original of this ship that Sir Francis Drake sailed around the world from 1577 to 1580. This full-size replica has done its own fair share of sailing, travelling over 140,000 miles (225,000 kilometres), and retracing in 1979–80 Drake's historic round-the-world voyage. Now permanently berthed, she is visited by thousands of visitors every year, a popular destination with children, especially those interested in explorers or pirates.

Continue along Clink Street and the **Clink Prison Museum** will be on your left. This murky museum is located on the site of a notorious old prison that dates back to the 12th century. Once owned by the Bishops of Winchester (who lived in a palace just to the east of the museum – now a ruin), it became known as the 'Clink' in the 15th century, but closed down in 1780. No trace remains of the bishops' palace except a lovely rose window – minus its glass. The prison museum illustrates the building's sorry history, with inmates that included a mix of prostitutes, debtors and priests. There are hands-on displays of torture instruments, which are great fun for children.

Golden Hinde
Opening times: 10am–5pm daily (Nov–Mar), 10am–6pm daily (Apr–Oct)
Admission charges
www.goldenhinde.co.uk

Clink Prison Museum
Opening times: 10am–9pm daily (Jul-Sep); 10am–6pm Mon–Fri, 10am–7.30pm Sat–Sun (Oct–Jun)
Admission charges
www.clink.co.uk
Tel: 020-7403 0900

Winchester Palace ruins

Southwark

The Anchor

Continue along Clink Street and go under the railway bridge, then turn right onto Bank End and The Anchor will be on the corner on your left. This famous riverside pub has been popular for centuries. It commands excellent views of the river. Dating from shortly after the Southwark fire of 1676, the present building is 18th-century, but traces of much earlier pubs have been found underneath it. The inn was at one time connected to a brewery across the road which belonged to Henry Thrale, a close friend of Dr Johnson's.

The Anchor
Opening times: 11am–11pm daily
www.greeneking-pubs.co.uk/pubs/greater-london/anchor-bankside
Tel: 020-7407 1577

Shakespeare's Globe

Take the riverside walkway past Southwark Bridge and you will come to Bankside, where you will see Shakespeare's Globe on your left. This is an impressive reconstruction of the Elizabethan theatre where many of William Shakespeare's plays were first performed. The circular, wooden structure is open in the middle, leaving some of the audience exposed to the elements. (Those holding seat tickets do have a roof over their heads.) It hosts open-air performances in the summer and an exhibition all year round, with an

Shakespeare's Globe

informative tour for visitors. Groups may also book to take a look at the foundations of the nearby Rose Theatre, or simply relax in the Swan restaurant and bar which is spread over two floors and has stunning views of the Thames and St Paul's Cathedral.

Shakespeare's Globe
Tours: 9.30am–5pm daily
Admission charges
www.shakespearesglobe.com
Tel: 020-7902 1400
Box office: 020-7401 9919

Cardinal's Wharf ⓫

Located just past Shakespeare's Globe is Cardinal's Wharf, a small terrace of charming 17th-century houses that has somehow managed to survive the centuries intact. A plaque commemorates Christopher Wren's staying here while building St Paul's Cathedral, which can be seen across the river. Wren would thus have had a particularly fine view of the building as it progressed. The name is thought to honour Cardinal Wolsey, who was also Bishop of Winchester and would have lived in the bishop's palace that used to be located near here.

Cardinal's Wharf

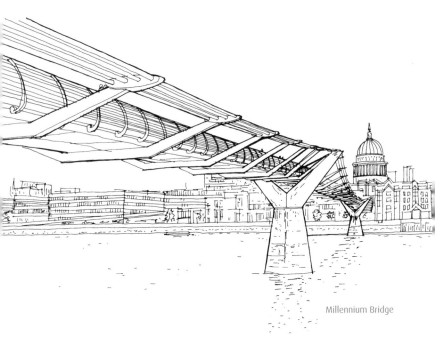

Millennium Bridge

Millennium Bridge ⑫

The Millennium Bridge, officially known as the London Millennium Footbridge, is a steel suspension bridge that links Bankside to the City. Opened in 2000, it was immediately nicknamed the 'Wobbly Bridge' because of an uncomfortable swaying motion that could be felt while on it. The bridge was closed for almost two years while modifications were made to stabilise it. Designed by Arup, Foster and Partners and Sir Anthony Caro, the bridge's suspension system has cables *below* the deck, which gives it a very shallow profile and improves the views. The 325-metre-long bridge is aligned on axis with the dome of St Paul's, thus giving the city a striking new view: the contrast between the high-tech steel cables of the bridge and the magnificent stone dome in the distance.

Tate Modern ⑬

This monumental temple to art began life as a power station. Bankside Power Station was designed by Sir Giles Gilbert Scott in 1947, a masterpiece of industrial architecture – functional yet wonderfully stylish. The power it exudes is an entirely appropriate expression of the function it housed. And the decision to save the building by turning it into a cutting-edge art gallery in 1994 was sheer genius. Some of the world's greatest architects were asked to submit proposals – one of which was the rather unimaginative idea of knocking the whole thing down.

Swiss architects Herzog and de Meuron won the commission in 1995, with their clever design that proposed only the subtlest of interventions. The building therefore retains much of its original appearance – at least on the outside. Scott's brick façade, comprising more than 4.2 million bricks, is

almost untouched, as is his landmark chimney; the architects' only alteration appears to be a simple glass box on the roof, running the length of the building, by which the upper galleries are provided with light. The interior, however, has been utterly transformed. The vast turbine hall – which soars seven storeys and covers 3,400 square metres (35,500 square feet) – now serves as an entrance lobby and exhibition space for super-size installations.

Until 2000, the Tate collection was shown in three galleries: Tate St Ives, Tate Liverpool and Tate Britain (in London; see Westminster walk). When the Tate Modern was opened, space was provided for an ever-expanding collection of modern art. The Tate Modern's displays are arranged into four thematic wings, each arranged around a large central room focussing on a key period of Modern art: Surrealism; Cubism, Futurism and Vorticism; Post-war Painting and Sculpture; and Minimalism. Many of the galleries are double-height, while others have wonderful views over the river. The architects' lightness of touch, combined with the handsome finishes and exquisite detailing, have created a museum that has justifiably become one of the world's best loved.

Tate Modern

Southwark

Behind, on Holland Street, where the original power station's switch house was located, sits the Blavatnik Building, which adds new galleries, performance spaces, educational facilities and cafes to the Tate Modern. Also designed by Herzog and De Meuron, it opened in 2016 and is named for the industrialist Len Blavatnik, who made one of the largest donations in the museum's history. The facades are in a similar brick to the main building but they have been laid in a lattice pattern which gives the building's monumental form a lightness of touch and makes for an elegant contrast to the rest of the complex.

Tate Modern
Opening times: 10am–6pm Sun–Thur,
10am–10pm Fri and Sat; admission free
www.tate.org.uk/visit/tate-modern
Tel: 020-7887 8888

Bankside Gallery ⑭

Just beyond the Tate Modern is the Bankside Gallery. This modern building, sitting in the shadow of its more famous neighbour, is the headquarters of two venerable British societies – the Royal Watercolour Society and the Royal Society of Painter-Printmakers – members of which are elected by their peers in a tradition that dates back over 200 years. Their work embraces both established and experimental practices. The gallery displays contemporary watercolours and original artists' prints, which are frequently changed, and many of which are for sale. There is also a superb specialist art shop selling art materials and books.

And for a magnificent view of the river and St Paul's Cathedral, drop in to the **Founder's Arms**, a popular pub at the water's edge, built on the site of the foundry where the bells for the cathedral were cast.

Bankside Gallery
Opening times: 11am–6pm daily (during exhibitions)
Admission free
www.banksidegallery.com
Tel: 020-7928 7521

Founder's Arms
Opening times: 9am–11pm Sun–Thurs, 9am–midnight Fri and Sat
www.foundersarms.co.uk
Tel: 020-7928 1899

Link to South Bank walk: Continue along the river, following Thames Path.

South Bank

Nearest Tube: Southwark Station
Approximate walking time: 2 hours

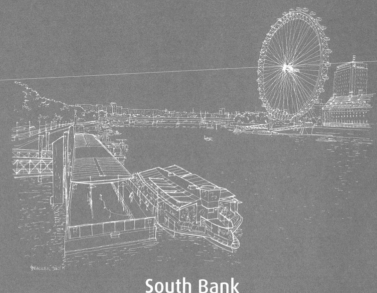

South Bank

Originally an area of wharves and factories, the South Bank was badly damaged by bombing in World War II. Following the war, it was chosen to be the site of the Festival of Britain in 1951. The Royal Festival Hall is the only building to survive from that time, and has become a hub of one of London's main arts centres, which includes national showcases for theatre, music, film and a major art gallery. Architecturally, this is not one of the most beautiful areas of the city, although the architecture is very good – certainly it was hailed as such by the architectural commentators of the day – but a lot of it is in the Brutalist style, which isn't to everyone's taste. The Royal National Theatre and the Hayward Gallery are important parts of London's cultural heritage. In Lambeth there is another famous theatre, the Old Vic, as well as some interesting buildings, including the Imperial War Museum and the Archbishop of Canterbury's London residence, Lambeth Palace. The South Bank also has some of the best places to take in views of the city centre, especially from the London Eye.

SOUTH BANK

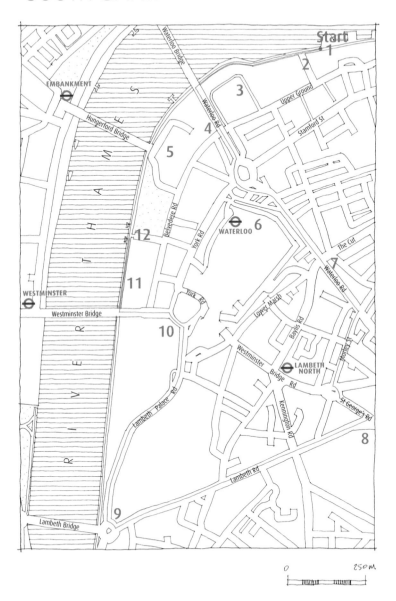

Start

1

2

3

EMBANKMENT

Upper Ground

Waterloo Bridge

Hungerford Bridge

Stamford St

Waterloo Rd

4

5

Belvedere Rd

York Rd

WATERLOO

6

The Cut

12

Waterloo Rd

11

York Rd

WESTMINSTER

Lower Marsh

Westminster Bridge

10

Bayllis Rd

Westminster

Bridge Rd

LAMBETH NORTH

Morley St

THAMES

Lambeth Palace Rd

Kennington Rd

St George's Rd

8

RIVER

Lambeth Rd

9

Lambeth Bridge

0   250 M

KEY

1. OXO Tower
2. Gabriel's Wharf
3. Royal National Theatre
4. The Hayward
5. Royal Festival Hall
6. Waterloo Station
7. The Old Vic
8. Imperial War Museum
9. Lambeth Palace
10. Florence Nightingale Museum
11. County Hall (former)
12. The London Eye

Imperial War Museum

South Bank

OXO Tower ❶

Leave Southwark station via Blackfriars Road and walk north in the direction of the river. Take the last turn left just before you come to Blackfriars Bridge onto Thames Path. The OXO Tower will be on your left.

This Art Deco tower was built between 1928 and 1929 by the Liebig Extract of Meat Company (they manufactured the famous Oxo beef stock cubes), incorporating part of the façade of a power station that stood on the site. Liebig wanted the tower to have illuminated signs advertising their products, but when permission was denied, he got the architect, Albert Moore, to instead insert three windows – one on top of the other – on each face of the tower, which happened to be in the shapes of a circle, cross and another circle – the OXO logo.

In the 1990s the tower was refurbished by Lifschutz Davidson Sandilands and turned into OXO Tower Wharf, which includes housing, a restaurant (on the 8th floor, with lovely views), shops and exhibition space. This is a delightful reuse of an old building, showing that with a bit of imagination even superannuated structures can face the future with confidence.

Gabriel's Wharf ❷

Continue along Thames Path until you come to Gabriel's Wharf. This riverside walkway has marvellous views of the city north of the Thames. Here you will find a pleasant little cluster of boutiques, craft shops and cafés. Their settled appearance belies the fact that this was once the centre of a storm over plans of what to do with the area after it ceased to be an industrial riverside. Locals strongly opposed the various office building schemes until a community association was eventually able to acquire the site in 1984 and built a co-operative housing block around the wharf.

Royal National Theatre ❸

Continue along Thames Path, past the London Television Centre, and you will come to the Royal National Theatre. Sir Denys Lasdun's Brutalist masterpiece was opened in 1976 – after almost 200 years of debate over whether there should even be a national theatre, and if so, where – as the last component of the South Bank arts complex.

The National Theatre Company was formed in 1963 under Laurence Olivier, after whom the largest of the performing spaces here is named. The three auditoria – a large 'open' theatre (with no arch framing the stage), a mid-sized 'proscenium' auditorium (with the traditional arch), and a smaller, experimental space with flexible stage and seating arrangements – offer a wide range of plays, from the classics to more cutting-edge fare. There are free evening concerts in the foyer as well from time to time.

Even if you don't go to see a play, the National is well worth a visit. Its concrete massing, though heavy, is actually quite well done; still it is best appreciated from afar, for, as with many Modernist structures, some distance is required to take in the crude sweep of its architectural gesturing. The urban landscaping is also good, although Brutalist concrete is not to everyone's taste. It certainly hasn't weathered well. The indisputable architectural highlight, however, is the foyer, with its multiple levels and terraces cut away to provide glimpses down through the floors and out over the river and the rest of the city.

Royal National Theatre
Opening times: 9.30am–11pm Mon–Sat
www.nationaltheatre.org.uk
Tel: 020-7452 3000

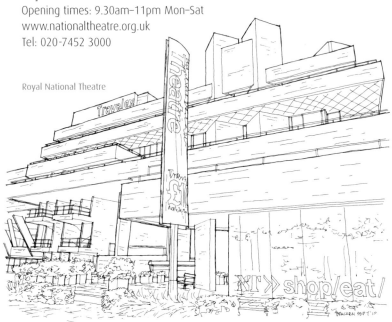

Royal National Theatre

The Hayward ❹

Across Waterloo Road from the Royal National Theatre is the Hayward, one of London's main venues for large art exhibitions. Named for Sir Isaac Hayward, a former leader of the London County Council, and designed by a group that included Dennis Crompton, Warren Chalk and Ron Herron, it was opened by Elizabeth II in 1968, and is another Modernist Brutalist behemoth. The Hayward's exhibits cover classical as well as contemporary art, with the work of British contemporary artists particularly well represented. The new foyer, by Dan Graham, was completed in 2003 and shows a selection of cartoons and artists' videos.

The Hayward
Opening times: 11am–7pm Wed–Mon (to 9pm Thur); admission charges
www.southbankcentre.co.uk/venues/hayward-gallery
Tel: 020-3879 9555

Royal Festival Hall ❺

Located behind the Hayward Gallery, and overlooking the river, sits the Royal Festival Hall. Designed by Sir Robert Matthew and Sir Leslie Martin, this concert hall was the first major public building built in London after World War II. Its impressive organ was installed in 1954 and there are also cafés and book stalls on the lower floors. A focal point of the Southbank Centre, it was the only structure in the 1951 Festival of Britain that was designed for performance. The London Philharmonic is one of numerous world-class orchestras that have performed here. The year 2004 saw the opening of Festival Riverside on level 1, which has new restaurants as well as retail, community and visitor facilities.

The **Queen Elizabeth Hall**, beside the Royal Festival Hall, and even closer to the river, is a more intimate concert venue. Its Purcell Room is ideal for chamber music. **Jubilee Gardens**, also beside the Royal Festival Hall, were laid out in 1977 to celebrate Queen Elizabeth II's Silver Jubilee. Formerly the site of the Dome of Discovery and the adjacent Skylon Tower during the 1951 Festival of Britain, the park contains a memorial to the British who were killed in the Spanish Civil War.

Towering over the Gardens is the **Shell Building**, headquarters of the oil company. Completed in 1963, it consists of a 27-storey tower designed by Sir Howard Robertson and three 9-storey wings. The choice of Portland stone for the cladding, and the bronze frames for the windows, was denounced by Modernist purists, but this more traditional cladding has meant that the building has weathered rather better than its 'purer' neighbours with their now grubby, stained concrete faces.

Royal Festival Hall
Opening times: 10am–11pm daily
www.southbankcentre.co.uk/venues/royal-festival-hall
Tel: 020-3879 9555

Waterloo Station ❻

Return to Waterloo Road and turn right. Waterloo Station will be on your right after the junction. Built in 1848 as the terminus for trains to southwest England, it was completely remodelled in the early 20th century, when a grand formal entrance on the northeast corner was added. Towards the end of the 20th century the station was enlarged again, this time to serve London's first Channel Tunnel rail link to Europe, the Eurostar. This moved to St Pancras International in late 2007.

Waterloo Station's concourse is spacious and lined with shops, cafés and bars, making it one of the more practical of London's rail terminals for those in need of more than just a place to transit through. The area around the station also has a good sense of community; the street markets around Lower Marsh are worth a stroll around.

The Old Vic

Continue along Waterloo Road and the Old Vic will be on your left at the corner with The Cut. This charming little theatre dates from 1818, when it was called the Royal Coburg Theatre, after the British royal family. The name was changed to the Royal Victoria in 1833 in honour of the young princess who would become queen four years later. Shortly after this the theatre became a music hall – an immensely popular Victorian form of light variety entertainment that included comedians, acrobats, magic and a host of other acts, some often quite bizarre. Lillian Baylis became the manager in 1912 and staged all of Shakespeare's plays between 1914 and 1923. This was where the National Theatre was first based after it was founded in 1963. In 1977 a charitable trust was established to secure the theatre's future. It then set up The Old Vic Theatre Company as its resident company in 2003. Renowned for the quality of its shows, it is also a popular venue because of its affordable seats and the pantomimes it stages every Christmas.

The Old Vic
www.oldvictheatre.com
Tel: 0844-871 7628

South Bank

Imperial War Museum ⑧

Continue along Waterloo Road until you come to Morley Street and turn right. Then turn left at St George's Road and **St George's Cathedral** will be on your left. The original building, which opened in 1848, was the first Roman Catholic cathedral in the United Kingdom since the Reformation and was the work of Augustus Pugin (who also designed the Houses of Parliament, with Charles Barry). Pugin was also the first person to be married in the Cathedral when it opened. Badly bombed in 1941, a great deal of the original design remains and has been incorporated into the rebuilt cathedral, which re-opened in 1958. St George's is the main church of the archdiocese of Southwark, which covers South London, North Surrey and Kent, and also the dioceses of Brighton, Portsmouth and Plymouth.

Across the junction of St George's Road and Lambeth Road is the **Imperial War Museum**. This museum used to be part of Bedlam (the Bethlehem Royal Hospital for the Insane), built in 1811. In less enlightened times visitors used to come to the hospital to watch the antics of the patients. The hospital moved to new premises in Surrey in 1930, leaving this large building empty. Its two flanking wings were knocked down and the central block converted into the Imperial War Museum, which moved here from its former home in South Kensington in 1936.

Sitting in impressive grounds, with two massive guns pointing up the drive from the main entrance, this museum contains numerous examples of war engines, including tanks, bombs and aircraft. There are also displays relating to the impact of war on everyday lives – things like food rationing, air raids, censorship and the ever important morale-boosting campaigns – which are far more interesting. The arts are also surprisingly well represented, with extracts from wartime films, radio programmes and literature, as well as photographs, paintings by Graham Sutherland and Paul Nash, and sculptures by Jacob Epstein. There is also a library with an excellent archive.

St George's Cathedral
www.stgeorgescathedral.org.uk
Tel: 020-7928 5256

Imperial War Museum
Opening times: 10am–6pm daily; admission free
www.iwm.org.uk
Tel: 020-7416 5000

Did You Know?
The word 'bedlam', meaning noisy chaos or uproar, comes from the nickname of the Bethlehem Royal Hospital for the Insane, which used to stand where the Imperial War Museum is today.

Lambeth Palace

Leave the Imperial War Museum by Lambeth Road and turn left. Follow it to the end and on your right will be Lambeth Palace, which has been the official London residence of the archbishops of Canterbury since the 13th century. Until the first Westminster Bridge was built in 1750, a horse ferry operated here, linking this side of the city to Millbank. The revenues from this ferry went to the archbishop. (He received compensation for the loss of this business when Westminster Bridge was built.) Lambeth Palace is not open to the public, but you can see large parts of it from Lambeth Palace Road. It is a particularly pleasing jumble of buildings, in a variety of architectural styles, some of which, such as the chapel and its undercroft, date from the 13th century. The gatehouse is Tudor, having been built in 1485. The palace has undergone frequent restorations since, but even the most recent was by Edward Blore way back in 1828.

Just outside the gates of the palace is the **Museum of Garden History**. Nestled in the grounds of the restored Church of St Mary of Lambeth Palace, it contains a comprehensive history of gardening in Britain, with exhibits of historical garden tools and other artefacts and curiosities. It also organises exhibitions, lectures and educational activities, and there is a shop stocked with a wide range of garden implements for those who feel inspired to try their hand at gardening. The church grounds contain the tombs of the two John Tradescants – father and son – gardeners to Charles I and Charles II, and inveterate plant hunters. There is also the tomb of Captain William Bligh, of the mutiny on the *Bounty* infamy, who lived on Lambeth Road nearby.

Lambeth Palace

Church of St Mary of Lambeth Palace

Museum of Garden History
Opening times: 10.30am–5pm Sun–Fri, 10.30am–4pm Sat
Admission charges
www.gardenmuseum.org.uk
Tel: 020-7401 8865

Florence Nightingale Museum ➓

Turn right onto Lambeth Palace Road and the sprawling St Thomas' Hospital complex will be on your left. Here is housed the Florence Nightingale Museum. The 'Lady of the Lamp' captured the world's imagination as the nurse who helped the wounded soldiers in the Crimean War (1853–56). She went on to found Britain's first school of nursing at the old St Thomas' Hospital in 1860. Though it is located in an obscure part of the newer hospital complex (near the entrance at the junction of Lambeth Palace Road and Westminster Bridge Road), the museum is worth seeking out as it gives fascinating insights into Nightingale's remarkable career, through displays of personal documents and memorabilia. The fact that she had such a picturesque name can have done her no harm (like that other great 19th-century heroine, Grace Darling, who saved 13 people from drowning in 1838). Lytton Strachey paints a less flattering portrait of her, however, in his hilariously mischievous *Eminent Victorians*.

Florence Nightingale Museum
Group and guided tours; admission charges
www.florence-nightingale.co.uk
Tel: 020-7620 0374

Florence's London: A Walking Tour
The Museum also organises a two-and-a-half hour walk through some of
the places Florence Nightingale lived and worked
www.londontowntours.london

Did You Know?
Florence Nightingale was a brilliant mathematician, who, in order to
illustrate her statistics to less able minds, invented the pie chart.

County Hall (former) ⑪

Leave the Florence Nightingale Museum and turn left onto Westminster Bridge
Road. The former County Hall will be on your right. This imposing edifice was
originally built as the home of London's elected government, the London
County Council, which subsequently turned into the Greater London Council,
and was disbanded by Prime Minister Margaret Thatcher in the 1980s. A
magnificent expression of Edwardian might and power, and a fitting seat for
the government of a city that ran the greatest empire the world has ever
seen, the main building is six storeys high and was designed in the Edwardian
Baroque style by Ralph Knott. Construction started in 1911 and the building
was opened by George V in 1922; the north and south blocks were added
between 1936 and 1939. It is now home to a leisure complex, which includes
the **Sea Life London Aquarium**, a permanent art exhibition, a Namco Station
amusement arcade, two hotels (the budget Premier Inn and the five-star
Marriott Hotel), restaurants and apartments. Parts of it can also be hired for
functions, including the impressive Council Chamber.

London Aquarium
Opening times: 10am–6pm Mon–Fri, 9.30am–7pm Sat, 10am–6pm Sun
Admission charges
www.visitsealife.com/london

The London Eye ⑫

Located at the riverside in front of the former County Hall is the London Eye.
Erected as part of London's millennium celebrations, it was at the time the
world's tallest observation wheel at 135 metres (443 feet), and immediately
became an icon. It has remained immensely popular ever since because of
the magnificent views it affords over the city centre. Thirty-two capsules, each
holding up to 25 people, take 30 minutes to make a round trip. The capsules

The London Eye

are made of glass and mounted on the outside of the wheel's rim to allow them unobstructed 360-degree views. On a clear day it is possible to see as far as 40 kilometres (25 miles). The London Eye's 80 spokes are made from a total of 6 kilometres (3.7 miles) of cable holding the structure in tension. Two cables, each 60 metres (197 feet) in length, support the structure from concrete bases in the nearby Jubilee Gardens. The Eye revolves continuously, moving slowly enough so that the capsules can be boarded while moving. It is halted for those requiring assistance.

London Eye
Opening times: 10am–8.30pm daily (weekends till 9.30pm) (Apr–Aug); 10am–6pm daily (weekends till 8.30pm) (Sep–Mar)
Admission charges
www.londoneye.com

Link to Westminster walk: Cross Westminster Bridge.

Westminster

Nearest Tube: Westminster
Approximate walking time: 2 hours 30 minutes

Westminster

Westminster and Whitehall have been at the heart of Britain's political life for more than a millennium. The first palace at Westminster was built by King Canute at the beginning of the 11th century, on what was then an island in a swamp, where the River Tyburn flowed into the Thames. The Benedictine Abbey church that was established half a century later by Edward the Confessor gave the area its name – a minster being an abbey church – and grew into England's most important place of worship. Westminster continued to be a royal residence up till the late 16th century, when it became home to England's parliament instead. Over the following centuries all of the major offices of state came to be established in the vicinity, particularly on Whitehall, the main road into the City of London. Yet, compared with most capital cities London lacks bombast – all the more remarkable considering it was once the capital of the largest empire the world has ever seen. There is little of the urban grandeur of Paris or Berlin, or the exuberance of Rome. The British Empire was in fact ruled from a not terribly grand-looking brick house in a small terrace off Whitehall: No. 10 Downing Street.

WESTMINSTER

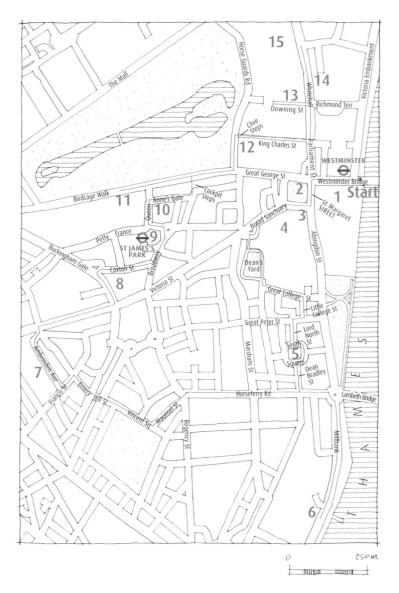

The Mall

Horse Guards Rd

15

14

13 Richmond Terr

Downing St

Whitehall

Victoria Embankment

Clive Steps

12 King Charles St

Parliament St

WESTMINSTER

Great George St

Birdcage Walk

11

Anne's Gate

Cockpit Steps

Queen

10

Broad Sanctuary

2

3

4

1 Start

Westminster Bridge

St Margaret STREET

Abingdon St

Petty France

Buckingham Gate

9

ST JAMES'S PARK

Broadway

Caxton St

8

Victoria St

Dean's Yard

Great College St

Little College St

Great Peter St

Lord North St

Marsham St

Smith Square

5

Dean Bradley St

Ambrosden Ave

7

Francis St

Emery Hill St

Vincent Sq

Maunsel St

Horseferry Rd

Regency St

Lambeth Bridge

Millbank

6

THAMES

0   250 M.

82

KEY

1. Houses of Parliament
2. Parliament Square
3. St Margaret's Church
4. Westminster Abbey
5. St John's, Smith Square
6. Tate Britain
7. Westminster Cathedral
8. Blewcoat School
9. St James's Park Station
10. Queen Anne's Gate
11. Guards Museum
12. Churchill War Rooms
13. Downing Street
14. Banqueting House
15. Horse Guards Parade

Houses of Parliament ❶

Leave Westminster station and follow the signs for the Houses of Parliament, which will be across Westminster Bridge Road.

Westminster Hall was built as a palace for King Edward the Confessor, on the site of King Canute's earlier palace, starting in 1042. Edward died in 1066 and his successor, Harold, was defeated by William the Conqueror that same year. Work continued on the palace between 1087 and 1100. In 1512 it caught fire, and after which ceased to be a royal residence, becoming home to the British parliament instead. The House of Commons was first established

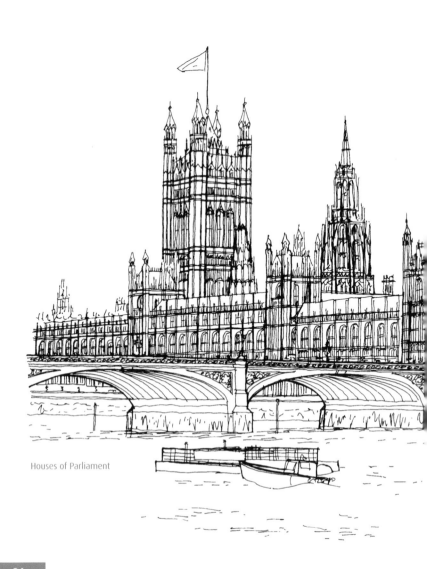

Houses of Parliament

in St Stephen's chapel in 1547 – and it was this that Guy Fawkes tried to blow up in 1605. The palace eventually did get destroyed – by fire in 1834. Only Westminster Hall, the Jewel Tower and a few cloisters survived.

A competition was held for the design of a replacement building, with the strict instruction that it had to be in either Gothic or Elizabethan style. Sir Charles Barry and Augustus Pugin were the joint winners. In spite of their differences – Barry was a Neoclassicist, while Pugin preferred the Gothic – they managed to work together to produce one of the highlights

of 19th-century architecture. Construction of this vast complex started in 1840 and took 30 years. The House of Commons was destroyed by a German bomb in 1941; Sir Giles Gilbert Scott designed its reconstruction.

Houses of Parliament
Guided tours (with afternoon tea optional)
Admission free but need to book in advance
www.parliament.uk
Tel: 020-7219 4114

> **Did You Know?**
> Big Ben is the 14-tonne bell in the clock tower of Westminster, named for Sir Benjamin Hall, the House of Parliament's Chief Commissioner of Works at the time the bell was hung. The clock's minute hands are 4.25 metres (14 feet) long.

Parliament Square ❷

Laid out in the 1840s to provide a more open aspect for the Houses of Parliament, which were being rebuilt after a fire, this pleasant square is not visited as much as it might be because of the heavy traffic that swarms around it. The square is often home to colourful protestors and there are a number of statues of renowned statesmen, including Benjamin Disraeli, Winston Churchill and Abraham Lincoln. Lincoln is located in front of **Middlesex Guildhall**, currently home to the Supreme Court. Originally a market hall, this current building was built by James Glen Sivewright Gibson in 1912–13 for the Middlesex County Council, in an odd but not unattractive mix of Art Nouveau and Gothic. It is now the final court of appeal for the whole of the United Kingdom for civil cases, and for criminal cases from England, Wales and Northern Ireland.

Broad Sanctuary runs from Parliament Square to the front of Westminster Abbey. Overlooking a smaller green between it and the Abbey sits the **Methodist Central Hall**, a rather grandiose example of the Beaux Arts style. It was built between 1905 and 1911 by Lanchester and Rickards as a Methodist meeting hall. The confidence and swagger of the building's architectural expression may be an effort to compensate for its being located opposite Westminster Abbey, one of the country's most famous and most beautiful buildings.

Supreme Court
Opening times: 9.30am–4.30pm Mon–Fri
Admission free
www.supremecourt.uk
Tel: 020-7960 1500

St Margaret's Church

Overshadowed but not overwhelmed by Westminster Abbey next door is the early 16th-century church of St Margaret's (it replaced a 12th-century place of worship). A fashionable venue for society weddings (Winston Churchill married his wife Clementine here), it retains some of its Tudor detailing despite having been much restored. A stained-glass window celebrates the engagement of Catherine of Aragon to Arthur, Prince of Wales (Henry VIII's elder brother). The Elizabethan explorer Sir Walter Raleigh is buried here.

St Margaret's Church
Opening times: 9.30am–3.30pm Mon–Fri, 9.30am–1.30pm Sat, 2.30–4.30pm Sun; admission free
Tel: 020-7654 4847

Westminster Abbey

Westminster Abbey is London's oldest and most important church, begun by Henry III in 1245. An abbey church had been established here as early as the 10th century by St Dunstan and a group of Benedictine monks; now it is the resting place of British monarchs, as well as the scene for coronations and other great pageants.

The Abbey was intended to combine the functions of three different buildings, all associated with Henry's brother-in-law, King Louis IX of France: the coronation church of Reims; the royal mausoleum at St-Denis; and the reliquary at Sainte-Chapelle in Paris. The tall, narrow nave – the highest in England at the time – represented the latest in 13th-century technology. The architectural style is French Rayonnant Gothic, but with a distinctly English accent. St Edward's Chapel houses the tombs of medieval English monarchs, and the royal coronation chair is located just outside. England's monarchs have been crowned on this relatively unsophisticated looking throne since 1308. The towers on the beautiful west front, completed only in 1745, were designed by Nicholas Hawksmoor. The north transept contains three chapels on its east side, which is where some of the Abbey's finest monuments are housed, while the south transept is home to the world-famous 'Poets Corner', with memorials to writers such as William Shakespeare and Charles Dickens.

Westminster Abbey
Cloister: 9.30am–4.30pm daily
Abbey: 9.30am–3.30pm daily
Chapter House: 10am–4.30pm daily
Cellarium Café: 8am–6pm
College Garden: 10am–4pm
Shop: 9.15am–6.30pm
www.westminster-abbey.org

Westminster Abbey

St John's, Smith Square ❺

To the left of the west front of Westminster Abbey lies a turreted building which contains an archway. Walk through this archway and you'll find yourself in **Dean's Yard**. This is private property, belonging to the Dean and Chapter of Westminster, and it is where **Westminster School** is located. The boys' school has produced more than its fair share of prime ministers, and this delightful cluster of buildings has the feeling of an Oxford college. On the east side of the square, a medieval house with a distinctive dormer window backs onto Little Dean's Yard, where the monks' quarters used to be.

Walk across Dean's Yard and exit by Great College Street; the **Jewel Tower** will be on your left. Along with Westminster Hall, this is the only part of the original Palace of Westminster to survive the fire of 1834. The tower was originally built in 1365 as a stronghold for Edward III's treasure and is now home to displays on the history of the tower itself, which served as England's weights and measures office between 1869 and 1938. The remains of a medieval moat and quay can still be seen beside the tower.

Cross Great College Street onto Little College Street and then take the next right onto Great Peter Street and then turn left onto Lord North Street. **St John's**, **Smith Square** will in front of you. One of the masterpieces of English Baroque architecture, this gem of a church has had an accident-prone history. It was built by Thomas Archer in 1728 only to be burnt down in 1742. It was then struck by lightning in 1773, before being hit by a bomb in 1941. It has since been restored, and is now mainly used as a concert hall. This entire area is a charming enclave of Georgian graciousness.

Jewel Tower
Opening times: 10am–4pm
Sat and Sun
Admission charges
Tel: 020-7222 2219

St John's, Smith Square
Not open to the public,
except for concerts
www.sjss.org.uk
Tel: 020-7222 1061

Westminster School

Tate Britain

Tate Britain ⑥

Walk around Smith Square and leave it via Dean Bradley Street. Turn left on Horseferry Road and then right onto Millbank. Tate Britain will be on your right after a few minutes' walk.

This impressive late-Victorian Neoclassical building, designed by Sidney R.J. Smith, is home to the largest collection of British art from the 16th to the 21st century. The permanent collection is displayed across three quarters of the main floor, with each room exploring a theme, or devoted to an artist; the remainder of the main floor and the lower-floor galleries contain the major loan exhibitions. The museum's restaurant has some wonderful Rex Whistler murals, which tell the story of the mythical inhabitants of Epicuriana and their expedition in search of rare edible treats. Of the many extensions that have been made to the museum over the years, the Clore Gallery is the most significant: a Postmodern masterpiece by James Stirling added in 1987, it houses a magnificent collection of landscapes by J.M.W. Turner.

Tate Britain
Opening times: 10am–6pm daily; admission free
www.tate.org.uk/visit/tate-britain
Tel: 020-7887 8888

Westminster Cathedral ❼

Retrace your steps to Horseferry Road and turn left. Follow the road until you come to Maunsel Street and then take a right when you come to Vincent Square. Walk along Emery Hill Street and turn left at Francis Street and you will be at the rear of Westminster Cathedral.

Westminster Cathedral

Built between 1894 and 1903, this is architect John Francis Bentley's masterpiece, and one of London's rare Byzantine-style buildings; actually it is in the Italo-Byzantine style, and was at pains not to be seen to be in competition with Westminster Abbey. This style was also a popular choice at the time because of the late 19th-century taste for Byzantine architecture, craftsmanship and symbolism, which were a feature of the Arts and Crafts movement. The busy-looking exterior of blood-and-bandage (red brick and white stone) owes much to Norman Shaw and Aston Webb, particularly the former's New Scotland Yard building on nearby Whitehall. Following the precepts of 19th-century theorists like Pugin, Viollet-le-Duc and Choisy, this was a 'truthful' building, one where the load-bearing did not depend on concealed iron or steel reinforcement. The tower soars 87 metres (285 feet) into the air, dominating the little plaza that opens onto busy Victoria Street.

The interior was initially left bare because of lack of funds, but it has since been progressively decorated using a variety of coloured marble. The nave is the widest in Britain, while Eric Gill's dramatic *Stations of the Cross* sculptures, created during World War I, adorn the piers. The organ is one of the finest in Europe and there are often free recitals on Sundays.

Westminster Cathedral
Opening times (tower): 9.30am–5pm Mon–Fri, 9.30am–6pm Sat and Sun
Admission charges
www.westminstercathedral.org.uk
Tel: 020-7798 9055

Blewcoat School ❽

Leaving the cathedral via the plaza, turn right onto Victoria Street and then left onto Buckingham Gate. The Blewcoat School will be on your right, at the junction with Caxton Street. Built in 1709 as a charity school, its brief was to teach pupils how to 'read, write, cast accounts and the catechism' – there is a colourful little statue of one of the blue-coated students in a niche over the centrally placed front door. This red-brick gem, with beautifully proportioned interiors, was bought by the National Trust in 1954, and now houses an upmarket boutique.

Blewcoat School
Opening times: 10am–6pm Tue and Wed, 12.30–8.30pm Thur,
10am–6pm Fri and Sat; admission free
Tel: 020-7222 2877

St James's Park Station ❾

Continue along Caxton Street until you come to Broadway. St James's Park Station will be on your left at No. 55. Built as an integral part of Charles

Holden's Broadway House – the headquarters for London Transport – it is notable for its elegant Art Deco massing, Jacob Epstein sculptures, and bas-reliefs by Henry Moore and Eric Gill. A small shopping arcade, also in delightful Art Deco style, runs through the building – feeling like a time tunnel back to the 1930s.

Queen Anne's Gate ❿

Exit St James's Park Station via Petty France and walk up Queen Anne's Gate. The street turns right just opposite Sir Basil Spence's **Home Office Building** – another Modernist insult to an otherwise graceful area; this behemoth squats like a malignant giant terrorising the pretty clusters of Queen Anne terraces. At the corner sits a well-preserved example. Dating from 1704, it consists of houses that look as if they could have been the model for the original doll's house. The ornate wrought-iron canopies over their doors are worth a closer look. Farther along the terrace is a group of houses built about 70 years later, many of which sport the signature blue plaques that announce famous former residents. The Victorian prime minister Lord Palmerston was one of them. Until quite recently the British Secret Service, MI5, was based here – allegedly. A small statue of Queen Anne stands just in front of the wall separating Nos. 13 and 15.

Guards Museum ⓫

Return to the corner of Queen Anne's Gate and turn right. Cockpit Steps – the site of a 17th-century cockfighting venue – leads you down to Birdcage Walk.

Turn left onto Birdcage Walk and the Guards Museum will be on your left overlooking St James's Park. The museum is under the parade grounds of the Wellington Barracks, which is the main headquarters of the five different Guards regiments. This museum uses tableaux and dioramas, as well as a fascinating collection of models and artifacts, to illustrate the battles that the various Guards have fought, dating all the way back to the Civil War (1642–48).

Guards Museum
Opening times: 10am–4pm daily; admission charges
www.theguardsmuseum.com
Tel: 020-7414 3428

Churchill War Rooms ⓬

Retrace your steps along Birdcage Walk and continue until the end; turn left onto Horse Guards Road. The palatial edifice on your right is the **Treasury**. This most important of government departments originally operated out of the Exchequer Receipt Office in the Westminster cloisters. Charles II moved it to Whitehall Palace in 1660. When that burned down in 1698 this new

Westminster

Treasury was built to a design by William Kent; a suitably confident essay in self-importance, it was finished in 1734 (Sir John Soane later designed an extension). It enjoys magnificent views of St James's Park.

Next door is the equally magnificent **Foreign and Commonwealth Office**. Originally home to four separate government departments – the Foreign Office, the India Office, the Colonial Office and the Home Office – this building was designed by George Gilbert Scott and finished in 1868, when the British Empire was entering its highpoint. Scott initially wanted a Gothic building but Lord Palmerston (then foreign secretary) insisted on a Neoclassical one – a style that would bespeak confidence and organisation, as opposed to the Gothic, with its hint of wild emotions.

Between the Treasury and the Foreign and Commonwealth Office lies King Charles Street, which is entered via the very grand Clive Steps. Located here is the entrance to the **Churchill War Rooms**, Winston Churchill's World War II headquarters. A claustrophobic warren of rooms underneath government buildings, this was where the War Cabinet – initially under Neville Chamberlain and then under Winston Churchill – met during the war. They include living quarters for ministers and military leaders as well as a Cabinet Room, where many of the strategic decisions that won the war were taken. With the rooms laid out just as they were when the war ended, it is possible to see Churchill's desk as well as various communications equipment and maps.

Churchill War Rooms
Opening times: 9.30am–6pm daily (Sep–June), 9.30am–7pm daily (Jul–Aug)
Admission charges
www.iwm.org.uk/visits/churchill-war-rooms
Tel: 020-7930 6961

Downing Street ⑬

Walk to the end of King Charles Street and turn left onto Whitehall. Across the road are the **Norman Shaw Buildings**. Originally called New Scotland Yard, they were built by architect Richard Norman Shaw between 1887 and 1906 as the headquarters of the Metropolitan Police. The delightful pair of Arts and Crafts buildings sport bands of red brick and white stone, and distinctive turrets – with ogee roofs – at their corners. A particularly fine complex, one that wears its architectural references lightly and well. The Metropolitan Police moved to a new building in 1967, and these have been used as parliamentary offices since 1979.

Located in the middle of Whitehall sits Sir Edwin Lutyens's **Cenotaph**. This understated monument, completed in 1920, is an excellent example of how to design a sombre civic monument, in this case to commemorate the dead of World War I. On Remembrance Day every year – the Sunday nearest 11 November – the Queen and other dignitaries place wreaths of red poppies here in a solemn ceremony that honours victims of both World Wars.

Norman Shaw Buildings

Continue along Whitehall and **Downing Street** will be on your left, all but invisible behind impressive iron gates. These gates were erected in 1989 for security reasons, and the street is no longer open to the public. No. 10 has been home to British prime ministers since 1732, when George II gave the house to Sir Robert Walpole. It contains an apartment, where the prime minister and his or her family live, a State Dining Room, where official guests are entertained, and a Cabinet Room, where government policy is decided, as well as some other sundry offices. (Prime ministers also have an official country residence, Chequers, a large country house in Buckinghamshire, which has been theirs to use since 1921.)

Next door to No. 10 is No. 11, the residence of the Chancellor of the Exchequer, while No. 12 is home to the Whip's Office – where the governing party plans its future campaigns. Downing Street is named after Sir George Downing (1623–84) who spent part of his youth in America, then returned to England to fight for the Parliamentarians in the Civil War.

Did You Know?
Sir George Downing, after whom Downing Street is named, was the second student ever to graduate from Harvard University.

Banqueting House ⑭

Farther along Whitehall stands the Banqueting House on your right (you can see an illustration of it in the Architectural Styles chapter). This was originally part of Whitehall Palace, which was built in 1529 but destroyed by fire in 1698. Inigo Jones's masterpiece, dating from 1622, is in the Neoclassical Palladian style, and when it was built it would have stood in startling contrast to the rambling Tudor turrets that surrounded it. Even today it manages to make its presence felt on a street where it is surrounded by architectural busy-ness (if not merit), not to mention the endless streaming traffic. Ionic columns and pedimented windows sit over a rusticated base, while garlanded swags link the Corinthian capitals on the second storey. Jones is credited with having introduced Portland stone to London, and it was here he used it for the first time.

The interior was planned to resemble an ancient Roman basilica and derives from Vitruvius via Palladio. The ceiling, painted by Rubens, depicts a complex allegory on the exaltation of James I, commissioned by his son, Charles I. Charles I was later executed on a scaffold outside this very building; 11 years later, in 1660, this is where his son, Charles II, celebrated his restoration to the throne. The building is still used for official functions.

Banqueting House
Opening times: 10am–5pm daily
Admission charges
www.hrp.org.uk/banqueting-house
Tel: 020-3166 6155

Cenotaph

Horse Guards Parade ⑮

Continue along Whitehall and Horse Guards Parade will be on your left. This was once Henry VIII's tiltyard (tournament ground) and now is famous for the twice-daily changing of the guard. These elegant symmetrical buildings, designed by William Kent and completed in 1755, overlook a vast parade ground with St James's Park beyond. This open urban space is a splendid surprise when coming off busy Whitehall at the edge of the park. It is the site of such colourful ceremonies as the annual Trooping the Colour, which commemorates the Queen's official birthday. For much of the second half of the 20th century it was used as a civil-service car park – this dreadful practice was stopped in the 1990s.

To the south is the **Old Treasury**, and to the north **Dover House**, home of the Scottish Office – both also designed by Kent. Past the Scottish Office, on Whitehall, is **Trafalgar Studios**. Built in 1930 as the Whitehall Theatre, its plain white façade almost seems to emulate the simplicity of the Cenotaph at the other end of the street. Inside, there is some fine Art Deco detailing.

Horse Guards Parade
Changing of the guard: 11am Mon–Sat, 10am Sun
Dismounting ceremony: 4pm daily
Tel: 0906-201 5151

Link to St James's Park walk: Leave Horse Guards Parade and enter St James's Park.

St James's

Nearest Tube: St James's Park
Approximate walking time: 2 hours

St James's

Henry VIII built St James's Palace in the 1530s, turning the area into the fashionable heart of London. It has retained its royal connections ever since, with Buckingham Palace, Clarence House (the home of the Prince of Wales) and the Queen's Chapel all nearby. The parks here are lined with aristocratic townhouses named after the great families who built them, such as Marlborough and Spencer. St James's is also home to Pall Mall and London's clubland, where major decisions about the running of the country are taken behind mahogany-panelled doors. Some of the city's most exclusive shops are also found here. Piccadilly, named after the ruffs, or pickadills, worn by 17th-century dandies, is home to such venerable establishments as Fortnum and Mason and Hatchard's bookshop, while just north of it lies Mayfair, still the most fashionable address in town.

ST JAMES'S

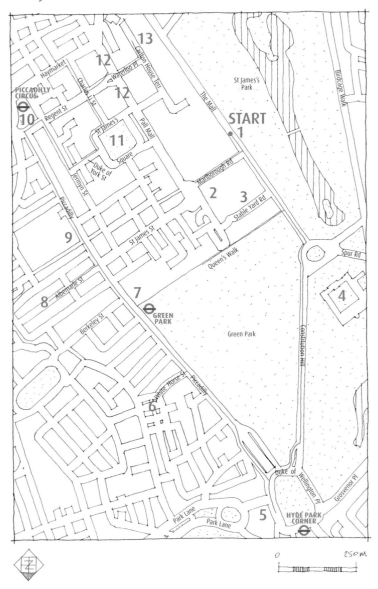

KEY

1. St James's Park
2. St James's Palace
3. Clarence House
4. Buckingham Palace
5. Apsley House
6. Shepherd Market
7. Ritz Hotel
8. Faraday Museum
9. Royal Academy of Arts
10. Piccadilly
11. St James's Square
12. Pall Mall
13. Institute of Contemporary Arts

St James's Park

St James's Park

Leave St James's Park station and walk up Queen Anne's Gate to St James's Park. London is famous for its parks, and justifiably so. This one in particular is delightful not only because it is one of the city's most ornamental, but also because of its proximity to Horse Guards Parade and Buckingham Palace, with the towers and turrets of Whitehall in the distance – providing tourists with some of the city's most picturesque views.

Originally a marsh, it was drained so that it could be incorporated into Henry VIII's hunting grounds. Charles II then redesigned it as a park, with, at the time, an aviary along its southern edge – which still sports the name Birdcage Walk. In summer, workers from the surrounding offices take their lunch or sunbathe between the beautifully laid out flower beds while tourists feed the ducks and geese on the lake. There are often free concerts from the bandstand.

Along the north side of St James's Park runs the **Mall**, a regal avenue that links Buckingham Palace to Trafalgar Square via Admiralty Arch. It was laid out in 1911 by Aston Webb, when he was redesigning the front of the palace and the Victoria Monument. It follows a path laid out in the time of Charles II, and has been one of London's most fashionable promenades ever since. The flagpoles that line the sides of the Mall fly the flags of countries of foreign heads of state who are visiting.

St James's Park
Opening times: 5am–midnight daily; admission free
www.royalparks.org.uk/parks/st-jamess-park/visitor-information
Tel: 0300-061 2000

St James's Palace

Overlooking the Mall on the north side of St James's Park is **Marlborough House**, currently the headquarters of the Commonwealth Secretariat. Built in 1711 by Christopher Wren for the Duchess of Marlborough, the house remained in the hands of the family for over a century, but was nearly demolished in the 1820s to make way for a terrace similar to the nearby Carlton House Terrace. From 1853 to 1861, it was home to various members of the royal family, and Prince Albert let it be used as the National Art Training School, the precursor to the Royal College of Art. After substantial enlargement in 1861–63 by Sir James Pennethorne, it became the home of the Prince and Princess of Wales. The house itself is in a not terribly attractive Queen Anne style, consisting of a symmetrical block over a raised basement, in red brick with some stone detailing.

Turn right onto Marlborough Road from the Mall and you will see in the wall of Marlborough House a charming Art Nouveau memorial to Queen Alexandra, Edward's VII's long-suffering consort.

On Marlborough Road is the **Queen's Chapel**, an Inigo Jones gem, built for Charles I's French wife Henrietta Maria between 1623 and 1627. It was the first Neoclassical church in England, and would have seemed shockingly plain at the time. Its design – beautifully chaste – seems to be a cross between a Palladian house and the cella of a Roman temple. The interior contains an excellent altarpiece, as well as gorgeous 17th-century fittings by Annibale Carracci. Originally intended to be part of St James's Palace, these buildings are now separated by Marlborough Gate.

Continue along Marlborough Road and you will come to **St James's Palace**. Built for Henry VIII in the late 1530s (who however hardly lived there), the palace saw more use by his daughter Elizabeth I, as well as during the late 17th and early 18th centuries. It is now the Royal Court's official headquarters, with foreign ambassadors still being officially accredited to the Court of St James's. The northern gatehouse, which can be seen from Piccadilly, is one of London's most famous Tudor landmarks, a mellow brick-and-stone blend of great charm and character.

Marlborough House
Only open during Open House weekend in September;
possible to arrange group tours; admission free
Tel: 020-7747 6500 (Commonwealth Secretariat)

The Queen's Chapel
Opening times: Sunday services,
all year (except Aug and Sep)
Admission free
Tel: 020-7836 7221

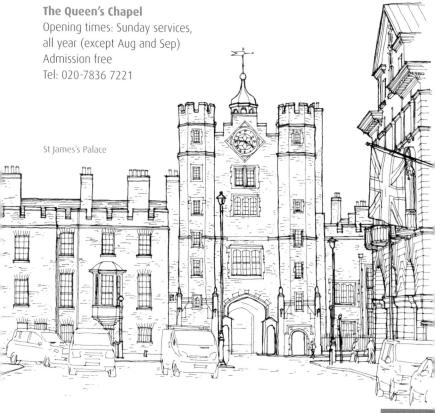

St James's Palace

Clarence House ❸

Return to the Mall and turn right; Clarence House will be on your right. Designed by John Nash and built between 1825 and 1827 for William IV (then Duke of Clarence), it later became home to the Queen Mother, from 1953 until her death in 2002. It then became the official London residence of her grandson, Prince Charles. This understated four-storey Regency house is rendered in pale stucco and has undergone extensive remodelling and reconstruction, particularly since being damaged during World War II. Little remains of Nash's original design.

Continue along the Mall and turn right onto Queen's Walk, which runs along the eastern edge of Green Park. **Lancaster House** will be on your right. Designed by Benjamin Wyatt and constructed of Bath stone, it was the last great Neoclassical house to be built in London, and for a good part of the 19th century was rated the most valuable private property in London. It was home to the London Museum from 1924 until shortly after World War II, and is now used for government receptions.

Continue along the Queen's Walk and **Spencer House** will be on your right. Built for the first Earl Spencer (an ancestor of Diana, Princess of Wales) in 1756–66, this is the last of the great eighteenth-century mansions in the city, John Vardy, a pupil of William Kent, designed the Palladian exterior, the ground-floor rooms, and some of the furniture; James 'Athenian' Stuart took over as architect in 1758, and the house became the first in London to make accurate use of Greek details for interior decoration. The house was converted into offices in 1956 and has recently been restored. Its lovely terrace and garden command wonderful views of Green Park.

Clarence House
Closed for renovations until Aug 2020
www.royal.uk/royal-residences-clarence-house

Spencer House
Opening times: 10am–4.30pm Sun (except Aug); pre-booked groups
Monday mornings; admission charges
www.spencerhouse.co.uk
Tel: 020-7514 1958

Buckingham Palace ❹

Return to the Mall, turn right, and you will be in front of Buckingham Palace. This imposing palace is used for ceremonial and state occasions, and is the official London residence of Her Majesty the Queen and Prince Philip, her husband. Three of their four children – Princess Anne, Prince Andrew and Prince Edward – also have apartments here. About 200 people work here in total, including the officers of the royal household and the domestic staff.

Originally built as the town house of the Duke of Buckingham in 1705, it was bought by George III in 1761 as a private residence for Queen Charlotte.

Subsequently, John Nash converted it into a palace for George IV, but both he and his brother, William IV, died before work was completed, so Queen Victoria became the first monarch to live here.

The palace forms a vast square around a central courtyard, with the east front facing the Mall added by Sir Aston Webb in 1913. This includes the famous balcony where the royal family wave to the crowds on the Mall below. The 19th-century interior designed by Sir Charles Lond – much of which survives – makes splendid use of brightly coloured scagliola and blue-and-pink lapis. Many of the smaller reception rooms are furnished in the Chinese Regency style, with furniture and fittings being brought from the Royal Pavilion at Brighton and from Carlton House (now demolished). The palace garden is the largest private garden in London and a haven for wildlife. It is overlooked by the lavish state rooms at the rear of the palace. The colourful ceremony known as the Changing of the Guard takes place daily from May to July, and on alternate days the rest of the year.

Beside Buckingham Palace, on Buckingham Palace Road, is the **Queen's Gallery**. This contains one of the finest and most valuable art collections in the world, with paintings by da Vinci, Vermeer, Monet, and many others. Entered via an impressive

Buckingham Palace

new portico, the galleries have been expanded under what has been the most extensive alteration to Buckingham Palace for 150 years. Changing exhibitions include fine art, jewels, porcelain, furniture and manuscripts.

Farther along Buckingham Palace Road are the **Royal Mews**. Designed by John Nash in 1825, they are the home of the coaches and horses used by the royal family on state occasions. The star of the show has to be the Gold State Coach built for George III in 1761, with its exterior panels painted by Giovanni Cipriani. The Mews also house the Irish State Coach, the Glass Coach, and the open-top 1902 State Landau, which carried Prince William and Catherine Middleton – Duke and Duchess of Cambridge – on their wedding day.

Buckingham Palace
Opening times: 9.30am–7.30pm daily (Jul–Aug); 9.30am–6.30pm daily (Sep); admission charges
Changing of the Guard: 11am daily; admission free
www.royal.uk/royal-residences-buckingham-palace

The Queen's Gallery
Opening times: 9.30am–5.30pm daily; admission charges
www.rct.uk/visit/the-queens-gallery-buckingham-palace

Royal Mews
Opening times: 10am–5pm daily (Apr–Oct); 10am–4pm Mon–Sat (Feb–Mar and Nov); admission charges
www.rct.uk/visit/royalmews

Apsley House ❺

Walk up Constitution Hill, and **Wellington Arch** will be in front of you. Designed by Decimus Burton, this monumental archway was originally built next to Apsley House in 1823, before being relocated here in 1883 because of a road widening scheme. Until that time the monument had featured a statue of the First Duke of Wellington; this was removed, and replaced in 1912 by a bronze quadriga. The arch is open to the public, and serves as an exhibition space. The viewing platform beneath the quadriga has wonderful views over London.

Overlooking Wellington Arch is **Apsley House**, also known as the Wellington Museum, as well as Number One, London. The original house was designed by Robert Adam and built in red brick between 1771 and 1778 for Lord Apsley, the Lord Chancellor. It subsequently passed into the hands of the First Duke of Wellington, who had defeated Napoleon at Waterloo and was soon to become prime minister. In 1818–19, Benjamin Wyatt undertook renovations, replacing the red brick with Bath stone, adding two side bays, and building the Waterloo Gallery for the duke's impressive collection of paintings by Goya, Velazquez, Brueghel and Rubens as well as furniture, porcelain and silver. The Seventh Duke of Wellington donated the house to the nation in

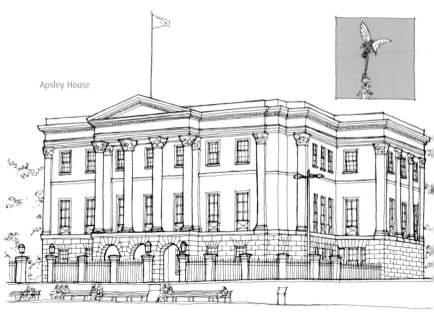

Apsley House

1947, but stipulated that so long as there was a duke the family could live there as well. Now run by English Heritage, the house is open to the public and contains a museum and art gallery. The Eighth Duke has an apartment in the building.

Wellington Arch
Opening times: 10am–6pm Wed–Sun; admission charges
www.english-heritage.org.uk/visit/places/wellington-arch/

Apsley House
Opening times: 11am–5pm Wed–Sun (Apr–Oct); 10am–4pm Sat and Sun (Nov–Mar); admission charges
www.english-heritage.org.uk/visit/places/apsley-house/

> **Did You Know?**
> Apsley House was given the nickname Number One, London because it was the first house visitors saw after passing the toll gates at Knightsbridge. Its official address is No. 149 Piccadilly.

Shepherd Market ⑥

Walk up Piccadilly and turn left at White Horse Street. Take the second left onto Shepherd Market. This attractive enclave of pedestrian-only streets is home to a variety of small shops, restaurants and cafés, many of them with outdoor terraces. It is named after Edward Shepherd, the man who built it in the middle of the 18th century. Until the 17th century this area was home to an annual fair which lasted for 15 days each May. The May Fair thus gave the area its name.

Ritz Hotel ➐

Return to Piccadilly and **Green Park**, which runs along the south side of the street, will be in front of you. This was once part of Henry VIII's hunting grounds and like St James's it was converted into a public park by Charles II in the 1660s. In contrast to St James's Park, though, Green Park has more natural landscaping, with fields of open grass dotted with clumps of trees. It was notorious in the 18th century for the duels that took place here. In 1771 a poet called Alfieri was wounded by his lover's husband, Viscount Ligonier, who then rushed back to the Haymarket Theatre to catch the last act of a play.

At the corner of Green Park and Piccadilly sits the **Ritz Hotel**, designed in a somewhat blowsy fin-de-siècle manner by Mewes and Davis in 1904–06, and named after César Ritz, the Swiss hotelier (who has been immortalised in the word 'ritzy'). The hotel's colonnaded facade was designed to be reminiscent of a French chateau, and also to evoke Paris, where the very grandest hotels in Europe were to be found at the turn of the 20th century. The hotel still retains its air of Edwardian potted-palm chic and is a popular place for indulging in the venerable practice of afternoon tea.

Green Park
Opening times: 24 hours daily

Ritz Hotel
Afternoon tea: Every two hours from 11.30am to 7.30 pm
www.theritzlondon.com
Tel: 020-7493 8181

Faraday Museum ➑

Continue along Piccadilly and turn left onto Albemarle Street. The Royal Institution, which houses the Faraday Museum, is at No. 21. Michael Faraday was a pioneer in the use of electricity in the 19th century; the collections in this museum include some of his scientific apparatus and personal effects. The work of other scientists is also featured on the three lower floors.

Return to Piccadilly and turn left; the **Burlington Arcade** will be on your left. This is one of four arcades of small but exclusive shops that were built in the area in the early 19th century (Princes and Piccadilly arcades are on the south side of Piccadilly, while the Royal Opera Arcade is off Pall Mall). Built for Lord Cavendish in 1819, primarily with the aim, it is said, of stopping rubbish being thrown into his garden, it is still very much in operation today, two centuries later, as home to purveyors of traditional British luxuries. The arcade itself is an ornately decorated space that is surprisingly light and airy.

Faraday Museum
Opening times: 9am–6pm Mon–Fri; admission free
www.rigb.org/visit-us/faraday-museum

Burlington Arcade, Piccadilly

Did You Know?
Burlington Arcade is patrolled by uniformed beadles who have the authority to remove anyone who offends the shopping public by engaging in such boorish behaviour as singing, whistling, running or opening an umbrella.

Royal Academy of Arts ❾

Next door to the Burlington Arcade sits the Royal Academy of Arts. Founded by Sir Joshua Reynolds in 1768, it hosts popular, large-scale exhibitions. The recently restored Madejski Rooms display the highlights of the academy's collection (which includes one work by every former Academician), while the Sackler Galleries, designed by Norman Foster and opened in 1991, host visiting exhibitions. The annual summer show, which has been held for over 200 years, exhibits over 1,200 new works; any artist, regardless of status, may submit a work. In the sculpture promenade outside the galleries is a Michelangelo relief of the Madonna and Child that dates from 1505.

The building itself – Burlington House – has a complex history. Begun in the 1660s, it was one of the first large private mansions to be built on the north side of Piccadilly. Its first incarnation was designed by Sir John Denham and in the ensuing decades was modified and added to by a string of architects, including James Gibbs, Colen Campbell and William Kent in the early 18th century, and Samuel Ware in the early 19th. The courtyard is a graceful public

St James

space off busy Piccadilly, and often crammed with people waiting to get in to see one of the prestigious exhibitions. Two shops adjacent to the gallery exits sell merchandise relating to current exhibitions; they also stock an excellent range of art books.

Next door to the Royal Academy of Arts is **The Albany**. Actually Albany Courtyard, this has been one of London's smartest addresses since it was built in 1803 by Henry Holland as bachelor apartments. Notable residents have included two prime ministers (William Gladstone and Edward Heath), the poet Lord Byron and the novelist Graham Greene. Married men were eventually admitted in 1878 but it was forbidden for them to have their wives here until 1919. Nowadays, women can also live in the building. It is not open to the public.

Royal Academy of Arts
Opening times: 10am–6pm Sat–Thur; admission free
www.royalacademy.org

Piccadilly ⑩

Farther along Piccadilly, on the right hand side, is **St James's Church** at No. 197. This church is said to be one of Wren's favourites among his creations. Dating from 1684, it has been much altered over the years (it was almost completely destroyed by a bomb in 1940), yet it manages to retain its essential character in the tall, arched windows and thin spire (a fibreglass replica of the original, erected in 1966). The interior is dignified and has quite a light touch. The screen behind the altar is one of 17th-century master carver Grinling Gibbons's finest. He also made the exquisite marble font – which features Adam and Eve at the Tree of Knowledge – and the carvings above the organ. The church maintains a full schedule of events, and has a popular café. The grounds are home to the popular **Piccadilly Market**, which is a food market on Mondays and Tuesdays and specialises in arts and crafts from Wednesday to Saturday.

Farther along Piccadilly, at No. 181, is **Fortnum and Mason**, one of London's premier provisioners. Founded by two of Queen Anne's footmen, William Fortnum and Hugh Mason, in 1707, this small department store holds a Royal Warrant as grocer to the royal family, and is famous for its luxury brands and delightful tea shop.

Next door to Fortnum and Mason is **Hatchard's**, London's oldest bookshop, and the second oldest in the country. It was founded in 1797 by John Hatchard, whose portrait can be seen on the staircase. Like its upmarket neighbour, this shop also holds a Royal Warrant (three in fact, from the Queen, the Duke of Edinburgh and the Prince of Wales). Popular with writers when they want to hold a signing, it also stocks a full range of what might be expected to be found in any bookshop.

At the end of Piccadilly is **Piccadilly Circus**, the hub of the West End. At its centre stands a statue, usually mistakenly referred to as Eros, the Greek god

Piccadilly Circus

of love; it is in fact Eros's brother Anteros, the god of requited love. Erected in 1892, it is a memorial to the Seventh Earl of Shaftesbury, the Victorian philanthropist. Originally laid out as part of John Nash's great plan for Regent Street, the Circus has been considerably altered, with most of the otherwise quite acceptable 19th- and early 20th-century buildings all but hidden behind vast advertisements and neon signs.

> **Did You Know?**
> Legend has it that a man was seen working his way diligently through *War and Peace* every lunchtime at Hatchard's for years. When he finally finished the book, they presented him with his very own, brand-new copy.

St James's Church
www.sjp.org.uk
Tel: 020-7292 4511

Piccadilly Market
Opening times: 11am–5pm Mon and Tue; 10am–6pm Wed–Sat
www.piccadilly-market.co.uk
Tel: 010-7292 4864

St James's Square ⑪

From Piccadilly turn right onto Regent Street and then right again onto **Jermyn Street**, one of London's smartest addresses for men-about-town and the shops they patronise.

Take a left onto Duke of York Street and St James's Square will be straight ahead of you. The statue of William III has dominated the square since 1808. This was one of London's earliest squares, laid out in the 1670s, and was popular with those who had business at court – the nearby St James's Palace. Most of the buildings are from the 18th and 19th centuries; they have had a number of illustrious residents, including Eisenhower and de Gaulle – both of whom were headquartered here during the war – as well as Nancy Astor, the Anglo-American women's rights pioneer. Chatham House (1736), at No. 10, on the north side of the square, is home to the Royal Institute for International Affairs. At the northwest corner is the charming London Library, a private lending library founded by the historian Thomas Carlyle among others.

Leave St James's Square by Charles II Street and the **Royal Opera Arcade** will be on your right between Regent Street and Haymarket. This was London's first shopping arcade and was designed by John Nash. Completed in 1818 it sits behind Her Majesty's Theatre (which was originally called the Haymarket Opera House). It opened about a year ahead of Burlington Arcade but has not fared so well over the intervening years; many of the traditional shops that used to be housed here have vanished.

Across Haymarket sits the **Theatre Royal Haymarket**. Distinguished by its enormous portico of six Corinthian columns, it was designed by John Nash and dates from 1821. It was originally intended to be part of Nash's plan for a stately route from the Prince Regent's home at Carlton House to Regent's Park in the north, via Regent Street, and represents a turning point when the elegance of Regency architecture was being replaced by the over-decoration that was to characterise the rest of the 19th century.

Pall Mall ⑫

Retrace your steps back to Regent Street and turn left. The street broadens out as it turns into Waterloo Place. The **Institute of Directors** is on your left at No. 116. Built by John Nash in 1827 as the United Services Club, this elegant building was the Duke of Wellington's favourite club.

Turn right onto Pall Mall and you will see a cluster of some of London's most famous clubs on your left. The name Pall Mall comes from a game called *palle-maille* – a cross between croquet and golf – which was played here in the early 17th century.

The **Athenaeum**, at No. 107, on the corner with Wellington Place, was designed by Decimus Burton, who though only 24 years old at the time, produced an elegant essay in restrained Neoclassicism. Burton was persuaded by the Club's founder, John Wilson Croker, to add a frieze based on the Elgin Marbles, which had only just arrived in Britain after having been 'rescued' from the Parthenon in Athens. It is a magnificent piece of workmanship, but some members were not happy about the expense, thinking that the money might have been better spent on an ice house (in the days before refrigerators ice houses were cold-storage rooms); this led to the witticism:

I'm John Wilson Croker,
I do as I please;
Instead of an Ice House
I give you – a frieze!

The Athenaeum

Next door to the Athenaeum are two clubs by Sir Charles Barry, architect of the Houses of Parliament: the **Travellers' Club** at No. 106 and the **Reform Club** at No. 104. These buildings' stately interiors have been well preserved since the time they were built (1829–32 and 1837–41 respectively). However, only members and their guests are admitted. The Travellers' has an Italianate theme, and many of its members, having made the Grand Tour, found it an amenable place to reciprocate hospitality to those they had met abroad. The Reform Club is modelled on the Palazzo Farnese in Rome and its magnificent interior is organised around a central courtyard surrounded by galleries. This was, in deference to the inclement English weather, roofed in glass.

Did You Know?
Both words in 'Pall Mall' are pronounced to rhyme with *gal*, not *gall*.

Institute of Contemporary Arts ⓭

Return to Waterloo Place and turn right. Then take a left onto Carlton House Terrace. The Institute of Contemporary Arts was established in 1947 to offer British artists the sort of facilities that were available to artists at the Museum of Modern Art in New York. Originally located on Dover Street, it moved to John Nash's Carlton House Terrace (which dates from 1833) in 1968. Its entrance is on the other side of the building, on the Mall, and consists of a large complex which is home to a cinema, auditorium, bookshop, art gallery, bar and restaurant. It also frequently hosts plays, concerts and lectures. Non-members may attend but must pay an admission fee.

Institute of Contemporary Arts
Opening times: Noon–11pm Tue–Thur and Sun; noon–midnight Fri–Sat
Admission charges (free on Tue)
www.ica.art
Tel: 020-7930 3647

Link to Soho walk: Walk along the Mall in the direction of Admiralty Arch.

Soho

Nearest Tube: Charing Cross
Approximate walking time: 2 hours

Soho

Soho is one of London's most colourful and cosmopolitan districts. It began life in the late 17th century as a highly fashionable address but went rapidly downmarket as the aristocrats moved farther west and waves of immigrants began to arrive: Huguenots from France in the 18th century and Chinese in the 19th. Gerrard Street is the heart of London's Chinatown, packed with excellent restaurants and bizarre little shops – it's like wandering in a Chinese city. Soho's first residents knew how to party and that tradition of pleasure continues today in the area's many restaurants, nightclubs and other entertainment venues, some of which are of a decidedly seedy nature. Soho is an extremely interesting part of town, with its wonderful mix of cafés and bakeries, pubs and restaurants, and is also home to some delightful old squares, as well as London's gay community.

SOHO

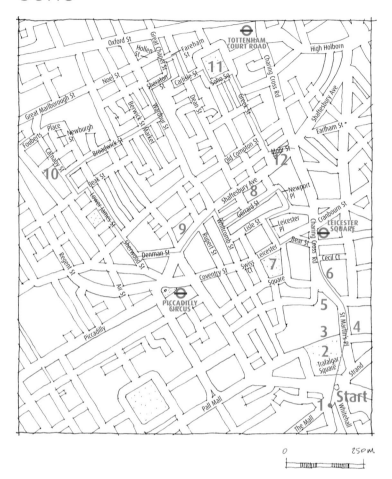

KEY

Regent Street

Admiralty Arch

Admiralty Arch ❶

Leave Charing Cross station and walk down the Strand across the south side of Trafalgar Square. Ahead of you will be Admiralty Arch, designed in 1911 as part of Sir Aston Webb's scheme to rebuild the Mall as a grand processional route leading to Buckingham Palace and the Victoria Monument. This Edwardian triple archway closes off the eastern end of the Mall from the southwest corner of Trafalgar Square. A clever piece of urban design, its two semi-circular facades address the streets on either side of what was an awkward site, cramped between Carlton House Terrace and the Admiralty. Vehicular traffic passes through the side arches; the central one is only opened for royal processions.

Trafalgar Square ❷

Trafalgar Square was laid out by John Nash in the 1830s and commemorates the Battle of Trafalgar, when Lord Nelson beat Napoleon's fleet in 1805. This is where London celebrates, particularly on New Year's Eve. It is also the city's main venue for protests and rallies. Parts of the square have been remodelled for pedestrian use, making it even more popular with tourists, especially the enlarged staircase leading down from the National Gallery. Nash's brilliant feat was to regulate into a formal and elegantly symmetrical design the crossing point of so many different streets and avenues.

At the centre of the square stands the 50-metre (165-foot) tall **Nelson's Column**, built in honour of Britain's most famous admiral, who died at the Battle of Trafalgar. The granite Corinthian column dates from 1842, while Sir Edwin Landseer's bronze lions were added 25 years after. The buildings that face onto the square fail to live up to the square's grand promise, though. On the north side sits the **National Gallery**, with its disappointing dome – far too small and undistinguished for a building of this scale. **Canada House** is to the west while **South Africa House** faces it to the east, neither of them particularly good. The **Grand Buildings** on the square's south side, built in 1880 as the Grand Hotel, have been recently restored and contain a pleasant arcade.

National Gallery ❸

Overlooking the northern end of Trafalgar Square is the National Gallery. Home to the national collection of art, the gallery has flourished since its inception in the early 19th century, when the House of Commons bought 38 paintings, including works by Raphael and Rubens. The collection was initially housed at No. 100 Pall Mall until this building was constructed on the newly laid out Trafalgar Square in 1832. Designed by William Wilkins, it is far from being

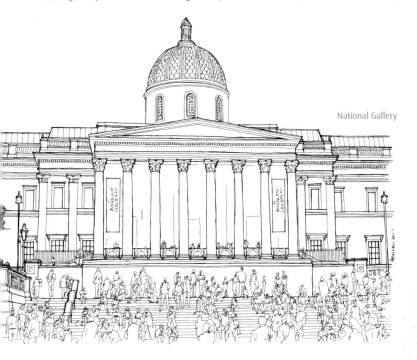

National Gallery

considered an architectural triumph. A building in such a prominent position should have a far more grandiose presence, while the under-sized dome looks more like an overgrown tea caddy than the crowning glory of the nation's premier art gallery

The collection, however, is magnificent, with over 2000 paintings from Western Europe. Highlights include the Rokeby Venus by Velazquez, The Hay Wain by Constable, the Leonardo Cartoon (Virgin and Child with St Anne and John the Baptist by Leonardo da Vinci) and The Ambassadors by Hans Holbein.

The Sainsburys wing was added in 1991 – to a storm of protest over Robert Venturi's Postmodern design. And rightly so. It looks even sillier now than when it was first revealed, its would-be witty gesture of the hodge-podge of Neoclassical detailing now a tired joke. This is home to the earliest works in the gallery's collection (1250–1500) as well as major changing exhibitions. It also houses the Micro Gallery, a computerised database of the entire collection.

National Gallery
Opening times: 10am–6pm Sat–Thur, 10am–9pm Fri; admission free
www.nationalgallery.org.uk
Tel: 020-7747 2885

St Martin-in-the-Fields ❹

Sitting beside the National Gallery, on the northeastern corner of Trafalgar Square, is St Martin-in-the-Fields, James Gibbs's masterpiece, and one of the most delightful places of worship in the city centre.

Gibbs was a Catholic. This meant that while he was ineligible for state commissions he had trained in Rome so his work had an edge over his contemporaries, who preferred to work from pictures rather than visit Catholic Italy. Gibbs's great achievement was to combine a Gothic steeple with a Neoclassical temple front, which he does with elegance. The tower and steeple were clearly influenced by Wren; in fact Gibbs took the building committee on a tour of Wren's City churches when he was submitting his proposals. The interior also echoes Wren, with an elliptical barrel-vaulted ceiling and saucer domes over the aisles. The plasterwork is rather good, by Giovanni Battista Bagutti and Chrysostom Wilkins.

Many famous people are buried here, including Nell Gwynn – Charles II's most famous mistress – and the painters William Hogarth and Joshua Reynolds. The crypt was used as a shelter for homeless soldiers and down-and-outs from 1914 to 1927, and during World War II saw service as an air-raid shelter. It also contains a café, a religious bookshop and the London Brass Rubbing Centre. Concerts are sometimes held at lunchtime and in the evenings.

St Martin-in-the-Fields
Opening times: 8.30am–6pm Mon–Fri, 9am–6pm Sat and Sun; admission free
www.stmartin-in-the-fields.org
Tel: 020-7766 1100

London Brass Rubbing Centre
Opening times: 10am–6pm Mon–Wed, 10am–7.45pm Thu–Sat, 11am–5pm Sun; admission free
Tel: 020-7930 9306

National Portrait Gallery ⑤

Across St Martin's Place from St Martin-in-the-Fields is the National Portrait Gallery. Overshadowed by its more famous neighbour next door, the National Gallery, this excellent gallery houses pictures of Britain's movers and shakers over the centuries and is well worth a visit. The oldest works are located on the fourth floor and include a Hans Holbein cartoon of Henry VIII as well as a number of paintings of some of his six wives. There is also a portrait of Shakespeare by John Taylor from 1651, and the famous Ditchley portrait of Elizabeth I. The gallery also hosts temporary exhibitions and film and drama events, and has an excellent shop specialising in art and literature books, plus a rooftop restaurant.

National Portrait Gallery
Opening times: 10am–6pm Sat–Thur, 10am–9pm Fri; admission free
www.npg.org.uk
Tel: 020-7306 0055

Charing Cross Road ⑥

Continue up St Martin's Place as it turns into Charing Cross Road. This whole area is a mecca for book lovers, particularly Cecil Court, on your right, which is lined with shops selling second-hand books and prints.

Charing Cross takes its name from the last of 12 crosses erected by Edward I to mark the funeral route of his wife, Eleanor of Castile, in 1290, which ran from Nottinghamshire all the way to Westminster Abbey. ('Charing' probably comes from the old Anglo-Saxon *cerring*, meaning a bend in the road.) Today a 19th-century replica of such a cross stands in the forecourt of Charing Cross station.

Bookshops, Charing Cross Road

> **Did You Know?**
> The cross at Charing Cross is considered to be the centre of London and is
> the point from which all roads are measured.

Leicester Square ❼

Continue up Charing Cross Road and turn left onto Bear Street. Leicester Square
will be at the end on your left. Inconceivable as it may seem today, this was
once a quiet residential square and was where Isaac Newton and the artists
Joshua Reynolds and William Hogarth lived. The square was laid out in 1670
and takes its name from Leicester House, a royal residence which vanished
centuries ago.

In the 19th century a number of London's most popular music halls were
established here, including the **Empire** (which is now a cinema and still sports
the same name) and the Alhambra, which was replaced by the gorgeous
Art Deco **Odeon** cinema in 1937. The **Hippodrome**, at Charing Cross Road,
began life as a variety theatre, then became a nightclub and is now a cabaret
venue. The **Trocadero**, on Coventry Street, attracts a younger crowd with its
gaming arcades, cafés, shops and cinemas. There is a booth selling cut-price
theatre tickets on the square, as well as a statue of Charlie Chaplin by John
Doubleday. The Shakespeare fountain dates from an earlier renovation in 1874.

> **Did You Know?**
> What can probably be counted as London's first public restaurant opened
> in 1801 in Leicester Square's Hotel de la Sablionere.

Chinatown ❽

Leave Leicester Square via Leicester Place on its north side and **Notre Dame**
will be on your right. Once a theatre, this interesting building was converted
into a church in 1855. The murals inside date from 1960 and were painted
by Jean Cocteau.

Turn right onto Lisle Street and then left onto Newport Place and you will
be in **Chinatown**, the main thoroughfare of which is Gerrard Street, which
is entered via a traditional Chinese gateway on your left. The Chinese began
emigrating to London in the 19th century. At first they concentrated themselves
in Limehouse, in the East End docks, and this is where the notorious opium
dens that were such a feature of Victorian melodrama were located. The
number of immigrants increased markedly from the 1950s onwards, and they
began to move into Soho, creating a new Chinatown around Gerrard Street.
This whole area looks as if it could be in Hong Kong or Shanghai. It contains
any number of restaurants, and odd little shops selling oriental merchandise.
Three Chinese gateways straddle the entrances to Gerrard Street, which is
a great place to watch the Chinese Lunar New Year celebrations, held each
year at the end of January or early February.

Chinatown gate

Shaftesbury Avenue ❾

Walk to the end of Gerrard Street and turn right at Whitcomb Street. Take the next left and you will be on Shaftesbury Avenue. This is one of the West End's main arteries and the pulsating heart of London's Theatreland – home to six theatres and two cinemas along its curving, sloping length (all of them, oddly enough, on its north side). The **Lyric Theatre**, designed by C.J. Phipps, is the oldest, having been in existence almost as long as the avenue. The street was laid out between 1877 and 1886 to cut through an appalling area of slums. It was intended to improve the traffic across this busy part of the West End. The avenue follows a much older roadway and was named for the Earl of Shaftesbury (1801–85), who did much to improve housing conditions for London's poor and was instrumental in getting legislation passed to curb child labour. A pub called **The Blue Posts** on Rupert Street is located where a pick-up point for sedan chairs used to stand in the 18th century.

Carnaby Street ❿

Leave Shaftesbury Avenue by turning right onto Denman Street, and turn right again at Sherwood Street, which runs into Lower James Street. Continue past Golden Square and walk all the way to the end before turning left at Beak Street. The next street on your right will be Carnaby Street.

In the 1960s the centre of swinging London, by the 1980s Carnaby Street was reduced to peddling tourist tat and trading on its once-famous name. More recently it has once again become something of a name in the fashion world, with the neighbouring area of Newburgh Street, Kingly Court and Fouberts Place home to some of the city's most vibrant young designers. Somewhat more sedate is Inderwick's, at No. 45 Carnaby Street, England's oldest pipe-maker, founded in 1797.

Walk to the end of Carnaby Street and **Liberty** will be on your left, overlooking Great Marlborough Street. This delightful Tudor-pastiche building

Liberty

was built in 1925 to house the famous shop. As an exercise in architectural time travel, this could have been a tacky disaster; instead it is a historicist gem, beautifully and sensitively designed. It was originally opened by Arthur Lasenby Liberty on Regent Street in 1875, selling oriental silks, and some of its first customers were influential figures in the London art world, such as John Ruskin, Dante Gabriel Rossetti and James McNeill Whistler. Liberty prints and designs epitomised the Arts and Crafts movement that took London by storm in the late 19th and early 20th centuries. The shop still maintains its strong links with craftwork, including pottery, jewellery and furniture.

Soho ⑪

Retrace your steps down Carnaby Street and turn left onto Broadwick Street. Continue to the end and you will come to Berwick Street. **Berwick Street Market**, which has been located here since the 1840s, is one of the West End's best street markets, with the freshest and most inexpensive produce for miles. Berwick Street also has some interesting shops – including Borovick's, which sells extraordinary fabrics – and an increasing number of cafés and restaurants. Its southern end narrows into an alley, which is where Raymond's Revue Bar has been presenting its Festival of Erotica since 1958.

Walk back up Berwick Street and turn right onto Broadwick Street. Take a left onto Wardour Street and turn right onto Sheraton Street which veers to the left into Great Chapel Street. Then turn right onto Fareham Street and right again onto Dean Street. Turn left at Carlisle Street and you will be at **Soho Square**. Laid out in 1681 – and originally called King Square, after Charles II, of whom there is statue here – this was, for a few years, the most fashionable address in London. The Tudor-looking building at its centre was added in the 19th century as a park-keeper's cottage. The square fell out of fashion in the late 18th century when the area became home to waves of immigrants. It was rehabilitated in the 20th century, but not for residential purposes; it is now mainly home to office buildings – which is a pity as the lovely mix of styles and scales make this an especially agreeable place to live.

Leave Soho Square via Greek Street and you will come to **Old Compton Street**. This is Soho's High Street, with its shops and restaurants reflecting the cosmopolitan nature of the area. It is also without a doubt one of the most delightful streets in this part of London. The Coach and Horses pub has been the centre of Soho's bohemian life since the 1950s, while there is a distinctly French flavour with places such as Maison Bertaux (28 Greek Street), known for its croissants and cakes, Patisserie Valerie (9 Marshall Street), known for its pastries, and the French House (49 Dean Street), which was frequented by Maurice Chevalier and General de Gaulle. The Algerian Coffee Stores (52 Old Compton Street) is one of Soho's oldest shops, while Bar Italia (22 Frith Street), another coffee shop, is located underneath the room where John Logie Baird first demonstrated television back in 1926. Ronnie Scott opened

Soho Square

his famous jazz club here in 1959, and nearly every great jazz musician has played here over the years. Old Compton Street is also the hub of London's thriving gay scene.

Berwick Street Market
Opening times: 8am–6pm Mon–Sat
www.thisissoho.co.uk/the-market
Tel: 020-7641 7813

Palace Theatre ⑫

From Greek Street, turn left off Old Compton Street onto Moor Street and you will emerge onto Cambridge Circus. The Palace Theatre will be on your right. Dominating the western side of the circus, the building is a typically late-Victorian mish-mash of decorative features, a garish confection of terracotta turrets and ornate glass. Built as an opera house in 1891, it turned into a more commercially viable music hall the following year. Now a theatre, it is owned by Andrew Lloyd Webber, whose musicals have held London and anyone else in the world looking for an undemanding evening's entertainment in thrall for decades.

Palace Theatre
www.palace-theatre.co.uk
Tel: 0207-492 1532

> **Did You Know?**
> The ballerina Anna Pavlova made her London debut in the Palace Theatre in 1910.

Link to Covent Garden walk: Leave Cambridge Circus via Earlham Street.

Covent Garden

Nearest Tube: Covent Garden
Approximate walking time: 1 hour 30 minutes

Covent Garden

In medieval times this area was occupied by a convent whose garden supplied Westminster Abbey, hence its name. Before the Embankment was built, the Strand ran, as its name suggests, along the river. Lined with aristocratic mansions, it was outside the cramped City of London, yet close enough to keep up with those who wielded financial power; it was also of course on the main road to Westminster, and thus close to those who wielded royal and religious power as well. One of the Strand's numerous noble residents, the Earl of Bedford, commissioned Inigo Jones to design a piazza for him in the 1630s. This was in effect London's first square and its west side is home to Jones's delightful St Paul's Church. The piazza turned into London's main wholesale fruit and vegetable market, up until 1974, when it moved out, and the whole area got a facelift. It is now one of London's liveliest districts, home to open-air cafés, chic boutiques and street performers.

COVENT GARDEN

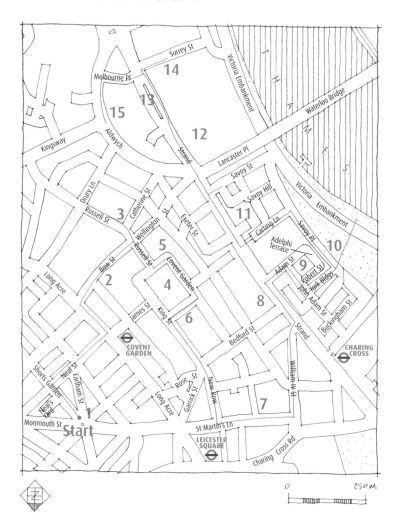

Surrey St

Victoria Embankment

Waterloo Bridge

Melbourne Pl

14

13

15

Kingsway

Aldwych

12

Strand

Lancaster Pl

Drury Ln

Catherine St

Russell St

3

Savoy St

Savoy Hill

11

Carting Ln

Victoria Embankment

Savoy Pl

10

Exeter St

Wellington

Russell St

5

Adelphi Terrace

Adam St

Robert St

9

John Adam St

Bow St

2

Covent Garden

4

Long Acre

James St

King St

6

8

York Bldgs

Buckingham St

Strand

COVENT GARDEN

Bedford St

CHARING CROSS

Shorts Garden

Neal St

Earlham St

Neal's Yard

1

Long Acre

Rose St

Garrick St

New Row

William St

7

Monmouth St

Start

St Martin's Ln

LEICESTER SQUARE

Charing Cross Rd

0   250 M

KEY

1. Seven Dials
2. Royal Opera House
3. Theatre Royal Drury Lane
4. The Piazza
5. London's Transport Museum
6. St Paul's Church
7. London Coliseum
8. Adelphi Theatre
9. Adelphi
10. Victoria Embankment Gardens
11. Savoy Hotel
12. Somerset House
13. St-Mary-le-Strand
14. Roman Bath
15. Bush House

Neal's Yard

Covent Garden

Seven Dials

Leave Covent Garden station and walk up Neal Street. Turn left onto Earlham Street and you will come to Seven Dials at the centre of the junction. This pillar – which actually has only six sundials, the central spike acting as the seventh – is a replica of a 17th-century monument. The original was removed in the 19th century, a time when this area was one of London's worst slums. Today it is a vibrant shopping and entertainment area, with streets and alleyways full of designer boutiques and quirky little shops.

The **Donmar Warehouse Theatre**, on Earlham Street, is a well-respected venue. It forms part of a shopping complex that was converted out of an old banana warehouse in the early 1990s.

Return to the Seven Dials and turn right onto Shorts Gardens; **Neal's Yard** will be on your left. This charming cobblestoned enclave is dedicated to alternative and eco-friendly goods and produce. It is also home to the Neal's Yard Dairy, one of the city's best cheesemongers.

Royal Opera House

Leave Shorts Gardens by turning right onto Neal Street, and then left onto Long Acre. **Stanfords**, at Nos. 12-14, was established in 1853 and is one of the country's best travel bookshops. It stocks maps, guides and other travellers' needs.

Walk back up Long Acre and turn right onto Bow Street. This was the location of the Bow Street Police Station and where London's first police force, the Bow Street Runners, was established in the 18th century. The station closed down in 1992.

Taking up most of the right-hand side of Bow Street is the majestic bulk of the **Royal Opera House**, home to the Royal Opera and Royal Ballet companies. The first theatre was built on this site in 1732, but was destroyed by fire in 1808. The present opera house was designed by E.M. Barry in 1858, after a second fire. It is a distinguished, imposing building – though somewhat out of scale in this narrow street, like a government minister condemned to a flight in economy class. The portico frieze, by John Flaxman, is rather fine; it depicts tragedy and comedy, and is a survivor from the 1809 building.

The Royal Opera House was where the British premiere of Richard Wagner's *Ring* cycle was performed in 1892; the conductor was Gustav Mahler. But it has also seen sadder days, being used as a government storehouse during World War I. Recently restored and significantly extended – a second auditorium and new rehearsal rooms added – it makes for a very grand evening out, although hardly a cheap one.

Royal Opera House
www.roh.org.uk
Tel: 020-7240 1200

Theatre Royal Drury Lane ❸

Continue along Bow Street and turn left onto Russell Street; the Theatre Royal Drury Lane will be on your righ. The theatre is called the Theatre Royal Drury Lane but its entrance is actually on Catherine Street. There has been a theatre here since 1663, making it London's oldest. In those days it was one of only two venues where drama could legally be performed in London. Three incarnations have been built here and all of them have burned down (including one by Christopher Wren). The present theatre, by Benjamin Wyatt, was completed in 1812, and contains one of London's largest auditoria. Famous for its pantomimes in the 19th century, it now stages big-ticket musicals.

Theatre Royal Drury Lane
www.lwtheatres.co.uk/theatres/theatre-royal-drury-lane
Tel: 0844-412 4660

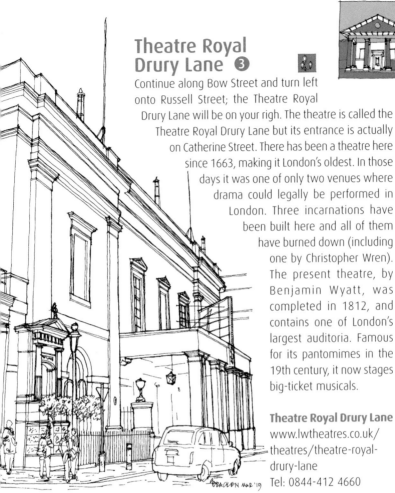

The Piazza ❹

Retrace your steps along Russell Street and follow it to the end where you will come to the Piazza at Covent Garden. Entertainment has a long and respected history here – the diarist Samuel Pepys wrote of watching a Punch and Judy show under the portico of St Paul's Church in 1662. Performers of every conceivable kind – and some of them that are beyond belief – can be seen here. The Piazza was the brainchild of the Earl of Bedford, who got Inigo Jones to plan an elegant residential square, modelled on the piazza at Livorno, in northern Italy.

Today, Jones's buildings are mostly gone, most of the Piazza is Victorian, and the square has been taken over by a large covered market. Originally a market for fruit and vegetable wholesalers, it is now home to a variety of small shops selling clothes, books, antiques and arts and crafts, as well as any number of places to eat and drink. The market's magnificent glass-and-iron roof anticipated the giant railway stations later in the century. On the Piazza's

Covent Garden

north side, the colonnade of Bedford Chambers gives an idea of what Jones's plan might have looked like – even though this is not original, having been rebuilt and partially modified in 1879.

London's Transport Museum ⑤

Located in the southeast corner of the Piazza is the London's Transport Museum, housed in a former flower market. The museum showcases the history of London's public transport, and also an excellent collection of 20th-century commercial art. London's public transport companies were always prolific patrons of the contemporary arts; these include the groundbreaking Art Deco designs of E. McKnight Kauffer, as well as work by artists such as Graham Sutherland and Paul Nash in the 1930s. Copies of some of these lovely posters can be bought in the museum shop. The museum has many hands-on exhibits; children can have a go at seeing what it is like to drive a London bus or underground train.

London's Transport Museum
Opening times: 10am–6pm daily; admission charges
www.ltmuseum.co.uk
Tel: 020-7379 6344

St Paul's Church ⑥

On the other side of the Piazza from the London's Transport Museum is St Paul's Church. Also known as the Actors' Church, it houses numerous plaques commemorating well-known thespians from earlier days. The austere portico facing out onto the Piazza is in fact the rear of the church; the entrance is on a courtyard off Bedford Street. Inigo Jones's initial design placed the church's main entrance facing east out onto the Piazza, with the altar therefore being in the west of the church. The clergy balked at such a sacrilegious arrangement and Jones was obliged to conform to tradition. He changed the location of the main entrance and the altar but otherwise left his original design intact. The portico's columns are in the Vitruvian Tuscan order; their strictness somewhat anticipates 18th-century Neoclassicism. The interior was destroyed by fire in 1795 but was rebuilt in Jones's simple, spacious style. A 17th-century carving by Grinling Gibbons on the west screen acts as a memorial to the architect.

Leave the Piazza via King Street and turn right onto Garrick Street. Rose Street will be the first on your right. Short and narrow, it slopes upwards

St Paul's Church

towards the **Lamb and Flag**. Parts of this building date from 1623, making it one of London's oldest pubs. The old-fashioned bar has escaped modernisation. It is popular with people working in this part of the city – in fine weather they drink in the pleasant courtyard. The upstairs bar is named after John Dryden, who was attacked here in 1679 by thugs – hired by no less a personage than Charles II, to punish the poet for having written a satirical verse about one of his mistresses, the Duchess of Portsmouth.

Return to Garrick Street and turn right; the **Garrick Club** will be on your left. Founded in 1831, it was named in honour of the actor David Garrick. The building is in a relatively restrained Italianate Victorian style, and its three storeys have been rendered in a grey plaster – which was intended to make it look like stone, but only succeeded in making it look dull. Popular with London's theatre set, this members' club holds an important collection of documents, manuscripts, paintings and drawings relating to the theatre.

St Paul's Church
Opening times: 8.30am–5.30pm Mon–Fri; 9am–1pm Sun; admission free
www.actorschurch.org
Tel: 020-7836 5221

London Coliseum ❼

Retrace your steps down Garrick Street and turn right onto New Row. Then turn left onto St Martin's Lane, and near the end of the street will be the London Coliseum – home of the English National Opera. This architectural extravaganza, topped with its signature globe, is one of the city's largest theatres as well as one of its most elaborate. Designed by Frank Matcham in 1904, it began life as a music hall, which explains its somewhat over-elaborate interior, full of gilding, purple curtains and plump cherubs. It was the first theatre in London to boast a revolving stage, and the first in Europe to have lifts. The top floor gives a wonderful view of Trafalgar Square.

London Coliseum
www.londoncoliseum.org
Tel: 020-7845 9300

English National Opera
www.eno.org
Tel: 020-7836 0111

Adelphi Theatre ❽

Continue down St Martin's Lane and turn left onto William IV Street and then left again when you meet the Strand. The Adelphi Theatre will be on your left. A beautiful Art Deco building, the Adelphi was remodelled in 1930 by Ernest Schaufelburg. There has been a theatre on this site since 1806, when John Scott, a wealthy businessman, set up the Sans Pareil Theatre in an attempt to launch his daughter's stage career – a woman who seems to have remained untouched by that fickle muse, fame. After having gone through several refurbishments, as well as name changes, and having narrowly escaped demolition in the 1960s, the theatre now stages popular musicals.

Adelphi Theatre
www.lwtheatres.co.uk/theatres/adelphi
Tel: 020-7087 7753

Adelphi ❾

Continue along the Strand and turn right onto Adam Street. The Adelphi, an Art Deco office block, will be on the right at the corner of John Adam Street. Its entrance has some fine bas-reliefs featuring workers at toil by N.A. Trent. This building replaced an elegant riverside apartment complex designed in the Palladian style by the brothers Robert and John Adam in 1772. (The name Adelphi is a pun on the Greek *adelphoi*, 'brothers'.)

The Adams also gave their names to this cluster of quiet streets nestling between the Strand and the river. A number of their buildings still survive here,

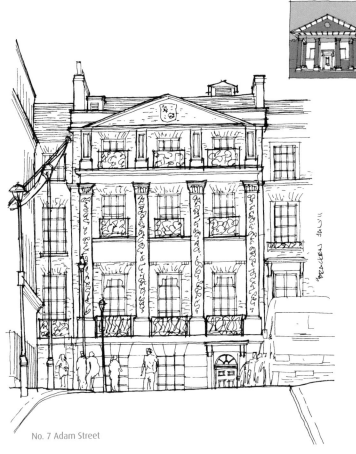

No. 7 Adam Street

notably No. 8 John Adam Street – the headquarters for the Royal Society for the Encouragement of Arts, Manufactures and Commerce – and Nos. 1–4 Robert Street, where Robert Adam lived for a time, as well as No. 7 Adam Street.

Victoria Embankment Gardens ⑩

Walk along John Adam Street and turn left onto York Buildings, at the end of which sits Victoria Embankment Gardens. This narrow park, created when the Embankment was built, contains meandering paths, well-maintained flower beds, and a number of statues, including one of the Scottish poet Robert Burns. There are concerts here in the summer. The park's oldest feature is the exuberantly Baroque stone structure in its north-western corner, at the foot of Buckingham Street. Originally a water gate to the Thames, built for the Duke of Buckingham in 1626, it now stands about 100 metres (330 feet) away from the river.

At the riverside across from the park stands **Cleopatra's Needle**. By far the oldest structure in London (though of course not native to the city), this was originally erected in Heliopolis in about 1500 BCE. Inscriptions on the pink granite celebrate the deeds of the ancient pharaohs of Egypt. It was presented to Britain by the Viceroy of Egypt, Mohammed Ali, in 1819 and erected here in 1878 shortly after the Embankment was finished. It has a twin located behind the Metropolitan Museum of Art in New York. The bronze sphinxes are not Egyptian and were added in 1882. The monument's base contains a Victorian time capsule with artefacts of the day: newspapers, a rail timetable and photographs of 12 famed Victorian beauties.

Victoria Embankment Gardens
Opening times: 7.30am–dusk Mon–Fri, 8am–dusk Sat and Sun
Tel: 020-7641 2000

Savoy Hotel ⓫

Return to Victoria Embankment Gardens and exit it via Savoy Place. Turn left onto Carting Lane and follow the street all the way to the top, where it narrows into a small steep lane opening out onto the Strand. Turn right and the Savoy Hotel will be on your right, down its own private street.

This is one of the world's most famous luxury hotels, built in 1889 by Thomas Edward Collcutt for Richard D'Oyly Carte (producer of the hugely successful Gilbert and Sullivan operettas). It underwent major renovations in 2008–2010 – which went considerably over budget because as they peeled away the hotel's famous Art Deco interior they found a magnificent Edwardian one underneath. They have made clever use of both as decorative themes for the hotel's various rooms, suites and public areas. The first hotel, built in 1889, was on the site of the medieval Savoy Palace and was a pioneer in the use of en-suite bathrooms and electric lighting.

Attached to the hotel are the **Savoy Theatre** (also built for Richard D'Oyly Carte and the venue for many of Gilbert and Sullivan's operettas) and Simpson's-in-the-Strand, a legendary English restaurant.

Return to the Strand and turn right. Then take the next right onto Savoy Street and you will come to a peaceful little garden which contains the **Savoy Chapel**. Parts of the chapel's outside walls have been standing since 1512 – Henry VII set up a chapel hospital on the former site of the Savoy Palace in 1502 – but most of the building dates from the mid-19th century. In 1890 it was the first church in London to be lit by electricity, and in 1937 became the chapel of the Royal Victorian Order. It is now a private chapel for Queen Elizabeth II. On nearby Savoy Hill were the BBC's first studios.

Savoy Theatre
www.thesavoytheatre.com
Tel: 020-0844-871 7687

Savoy Chapel
www.royalchapelsavoy.org
Tel: 020-7836 7221

Savoy Chapel

> **Did You Know?**
> The forecourt of the Savoy Hotel is the only street in Britain where traffic drives on the right.

Somerset House ⑫

Return to the Strand and turn right. Past Lancaster Place, Somerset House will be on your right. One of Britain's great public buildings, this was built in the 1770s to house various civil-service departments as well as the Society of Antiquaries and the Royal Academy. In effect it was the world's first office block. Sir William Chambers's design for the building was in the style of Louis XVI, with magnificently crafted detail and plenty of internal drama, particularly the spatially adventurous oval and semi-circular staircases and the open loggias above rusticated arches. The building was extended in the 19th century, with wings to the east and west designed by Robert Smirke and James Pennethorne. The Strand entrance is a trio of tall arches, which lead, through a sculpture-filled vestibule, onto a magnificent courtyard, faced on all four sides by beautifully detailed facades. The courtyard, closed to the public for nearly a century, was revitalised by the architects Inskip and Jenkins, and now hosts classical concerts and, during winter, a delightful ice-skating rink. From the courtyard it is possible to stroll through the South Building – where the Admiralty Restaurant looks out over the Thames – and out to Waterloo Bridge.

Somerset House is today home to the **Courtauld Gallery**. This small but impressive collection includes works by Botticelli, Brueghel, Bellini and Rubens (including his masterpiece *The Descent from the Cross*), but is definitely best known for its Impressionist and Post-Impressionist gems – Monet, Degas, Renoir, Van Gogh, Cézanne. It also hosts temporary exhibitions throughout the year.

Somerset House
Opening times: 10am–6pm Mon, Tue, Sat and Sun, 11am–8pm, Wed–Fri
Admission free
www.somersethouse.org.uk
Tel: 020-7845 4600

Courtauld Gallery
Closed for renovations until early 2021
www.somersethouse.org.uk/whats-on/courtauld-gallery

St-Mary-le-Strand ⓭

Continue along the Strand and you will see St-Mary-le-Strand ahead of you – seemingly stranded in the middle of the street. Consecrated in 1724, this was James Gibbs's first public building (he went on to design St-Martin-in-the-Fields). Gibbs's work was to become immensely influential, particularly in America, where it became known as the US Colonial Style. Gibbs was, in his turn, influenced by Christopher Wren, but also by the Baroque churches

Somerset House

he had seen in Rome when studying there. This explains the exuberantly decorative detail on the church's exterior, which contains a many-arched tower, layered like a wedding cake, culminating in a cupola and lantern.

St-Mary-le-Strand
www.stmarylestrand.org

Roman Bath

Continue along the Strand and turn right onto Surrey Street, follow it to the end, then take a right onto Temple Place and another right onto Strand Land and the Roman Bath will be on your right at No. 5. This is not in fact a Roman bath at all – the Romans never settled this far outside the city walls of Londinium. This structure is thought to have been a cistern feeding the fountains of nearby Somerset House. It was open to the public in the 19th century, when taking a plunge in its icy waters was thought to be beneficial to the health.

Roman Bath
Opening times: 10am–12.30pm Mon–Sat
Admission free
Tel: 020-7641 5264

Bush House ⑮

Return to the Strand, cross it, and go up Melbourne Place. Turn left onto Aldwych, and Bush House will be on your left. Situated at the centre of the Aldwych crescent and on the axis of Kingsway, this elegant essay in 20th-century Neoclassicism with great urban presence was built as a manufacturers' showroom in 1935 by Irving T. Bush. Its imposing north entrance is graced by various statues symbolising the cordiality of Anglo-American relations. Used as radio studios since 1940, it was for many years home to the BBC World Service (which has since moved to Broadcasting House). The best views of it are from Kingsway.

Link to Holborn walk: Retrace your steps along Aldwych all the way to the Strand and turn left.

Bush House

Holborn

Nearest Tube: Temple
Approximate walking time: 1 hour 30 minutes

Holborn

This is the home of London's legal profession. Originally a suburb of the medieval city, it was conveniently located en route to the royal seat of power at Westminster. The lawyers built beautiful homes for themselves, arranged around leafy squares like Lincoln's Inn Fields. Here is where the Inns of Court (lawyers' offices) are located, conveniently close to the magnificent Gothic edifice that is the Royal Courts of Justice, where the Strand turns into Fleet Street. Fleet Street was until recently home to the country's press; most of the newspapers moved out to the less expensive suburbs in the 1980s. Holborn also used to be one of the city's main shopping districts, now, however, only the jewellers of Hatton Garden and the London Silver Vaults remain. A number of buildings in the district survived the Great Fire, giving a hint of what it might have been like here in Tudor times. Sir John Soane's eclectic museum is one of the highlights in this area, together with some interesting churches, including the 13th-century Temple church, St Bride's – the model for the tiered wedding cake – and the Wren-designed St Clement Danes, which is where the walk begins.

HOLBORN

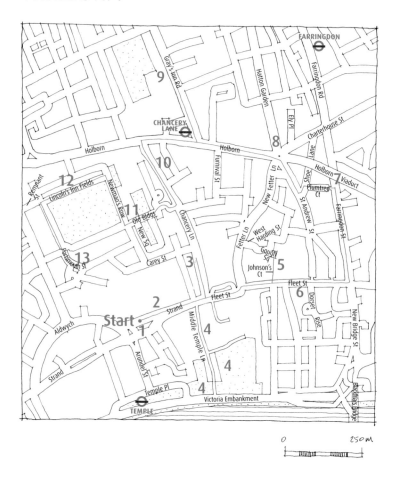

FARRINGDON

Gray's Inn Rd

Hatton Garden

Farringdon Rd

Ely Pl

Charterhouse St

CHANCERY LANE

Holborn

Holborn

Furnival St

New Fetter Ln

Lane

Holborn Viaduct

Shoe

Plumtree Ct

St Andrew St

Farringdon St

Holborn

Serpeant St

Lincoln's Inn Fields

Newman's Row

Old Bldgs

New Sq

Chancery Ln

Fetter Ln

West Harding St

Gough Sq

Johnson's Ct

Carey St

Portsmouth St

Fleet St

Fleet St

Dorset Rise

New Bridge St

Start

Strand

Middle Temple Ln

Aldwych

Arundel St

Strand

Temple Pl

Victoria Embankment

Blackfriars Bridge

TEMPLE

0   250 m

KEY

1. St Clement Danes
2. Royal Courts of Justice
3. Law Society
4. Temple
5. Dr Johnson's House
6. Fleet Street
7. Holborn Viaduct
8. Hatton Garden
9. Gray's Inn
10. London Silver Vaults
11. Lincoln's Inn
12. Sir John Soane's Museum
13. Old Curiosity Shop

Old Curiosity Shop

St Clement Danes ➊

Leave Temple station and walk up Arundel Street and St Clement Danes will be to your right in the middle of the Strand. Designed by Sir Christopher Wren in 1680–82, with steeple added by James Gibbs in 1719–20, this is the official place of worship of the Royal Air Force (even though St Clement is the patron saint of mariners). It takes its name from a church that was built on this site by descendants of Danish invaders whom Alfred the Great had allowed to remain in London in the 9th century. The church was a popular burial place for prominent Londoners from the 17th to the 19th century, some of whose memorials can still be seen in the crypt. There is also a stone tablet commemorating William Webb Ellis, rector here in the early 19th century, who is generally credited with inventing rugby in 1823. Outside the church are statues commemorating William Gladstone, the Victorian prime minister, and Dr Johnson, who often used to come to service here.

St Clement Danes is said to be one of the churches featured in the nursery rhyme 'Oranges and Lemons'; its bells ring out the famous tune every Monday to Saturday at 9am, 12 noon, 3 and 6pm, and an Oranges and Lemons service is held every year in March.

St Clement Danes
Opening times: 9am–4pm Mon–Fri, 10am–3pm Sat, 9.30am–3pm Sun
www.raf.mod.uk/our-organisation/units/st-clement-danes-church
Tel: 020-7242 8282

Did You Know?
The crypt of St Clement Danes has a chain hanging on the wall – said to have held the coffin lids in place, to protect fresh copses from being stolen by body snatchers for sale to medical teaching hospitals.

Royal Courts of Justice ➋

Continue along the Strand and on your left will be the Royal Courts of Justice, where the High Court of England and Wales and the Court of Appeal are located. (These are civil courts, dealing with divorce, libel and civil liability, etc.; criminal cases are dealt with at Old Bailey.) This massive Victorian Gothic complex, opened in 1822, is made of 35 million bricks faced with Portland stone. The Strand entrance consists of two elaborately carved porches with imposing iron gates. The outer porch features the heads of prominent judges and lawyers, with Jesus standing at its highest point, flanked by Solomon and Alfred the Great. Moses is featured on the northern front of the building, which also contains a sculpture of a fighting cat and dog, supposedly representing litigants. Each court has its own interior style – each designed by a different architect.

The statue of a dragon in front of the courts is the **Temple Bar Memorial**, which marks the border of the City of London. A large triumphal arch used

Royal Courts of Justice

to stand here but was removed in 1880 to improve traffic circulation. It is a long-standing tradition on state occasions for the king or queen to wait at the Temple Bar Memorial to ask permission from the Lord Mayor of the City if they may enter.

Royal Courts of Justice
Opening times: 10.30am–5pm Mon–Fri; admission free
www.nationaljusticemuseum.org.uk/venue/royal-courts-of-justice

Holborn

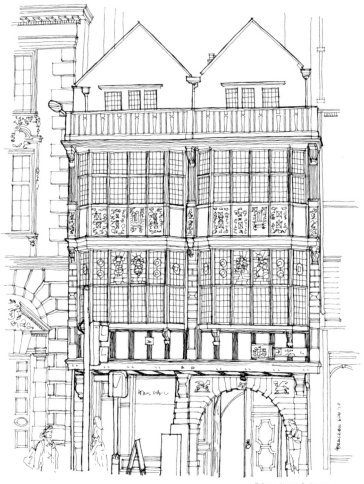
Prince Henry's Room

Law Society ❸

Continue along the Strand, which turns into Fleet Street. Turn left onto Chancery Lane, and the Law Society will be on your left at No. 113. This is a fine building, the main part of which features four large Ionic columns. It was completed in 1832. The northern extension – designed by Charles Holden, an Arts and Crafts pioneer who went on to design London's tube stations – features in its window arches four seated figures: Truth, Justice, Liberty and Mercy. The railings along the pavement sport a handsome series of gold lions.

Temple ❹

Return to Fleet Street and cross it. At No. 17 is **Prince Henry's Room**, an authentic 17th-century room inside a charming Tudor gatehouse. Built in 1610 as part of a Fleet Street tavern, the room's decorations feature the coat-of-arms of the Prince of Wales – probably marking the investiture of Henry, James I's son, as Prince of Wales (he died before he could become king). The building's traditional half-timbered front is original, as is some of the room's oak panelling.

The gateway leads to **Temple**, home of two of London's four Inns of Court: Middle Temple and Inner Temple. (The other two are Lincoln's Inn and Gray's Inn, a short distance to the north.) This beautiful complex consists of mellow-bricked Georgian buildings, detailed with creamy Portland stone, and arranged around a series of leafy courtyards, with lawns stretching down to the Thames. Temple derives its name from the Knights Templar, a chivalrous order who protected pilgrims travelling to the Holy Land. **Temple Church** was built in the 13th century and contains effigies of some of the Knights Templar in its nave. Initiations into the order took place in the crypt. A beautiful little building, it contains an unusual round tower and battlements and is constructed in a warm yellow-coloured sandstone. **Middle Temple Hall** has an original and rather fine Elizabethan interior, and was where Shakespeare's *Twelfth Night* was first performed in 1601.

Inner Temple
www.innertemple.org.uk
Tel: 020-7797 8250

Inner Temple Garden
Opening times: 12.30–3pm Mon–Fri; admission free

Temple Church
Opening times: 10am–4pm Mon–Fri; admission charges
www.templechurch.com
Tel: 020-7353 8559

Middle Temple Hall
www.middletemple.org.uk
Tel: 020-7427 4800

Dr Johnson's House ❺

Wander the courts and alleys of Temple before returning to Fleet Street and turning right. Then take a left into Johnson's Court and follow it until you come to Dr Johnson's House at No. 17 Gough Square. This was the home of the 18th-century scholar who compiled the first definitive dictionary of the English language in 1755. Dr Johnson's sharp-witted remarks have been preserved for posterity by his gifted biographer and friend James Boswell. Johnson lived here from 1748 to 1759, and it was in the attic that he and six scribes stood all day long at high desks working on the magnificent lexicon. The house was built before 1700 but is furnished in an 18th-century style and contains

Holborn

an exhibition of pieces that relate to Dr Johnson and his era. These include a tea set belonging to a friend of his, Mrs Thrale, as well as pictures of the great man himself and some of his contemporaries. There is also a selection of replica Georgian costumes which children can try on.

Return to Fleet Street and turn left; **Ye Olde Cheshire Cheese** will be on your left at No. 145. This is one of the few London pubs to have kept their original 19th-century layout (consisting of small rooms with fireplaces, benches and tables) instead of knocking it into one large bar. There has been a pub here for centuries and some parts of the building date as far back as 1667, when it was rebuilt after the Great Fire. It has long had literary connections and was where Pepys drank in the 17th century, Dr Johnson in the 18th and Charles Dickens and Mark Twain in the 19th.

Dr Johnson's House
Opening times: 11am–5pm Mon–Sat (Oct–Apr); 11am–5.30pm Mon–Sat (May–Sep); admission charges
www.drjohnsonshouse.org
Tel: 020-7353 3745

Ye Olde Cheshire Cheese
Tel: 020-7353 6170

Fleet Street ⑥

For centuries Fleet Street was home to Britain's press. Since the 1980s, however, most of the newspapers and press agencies have moved to larger premises in other parts of the city; the last major news office, Reuters, moved out in 2005. Named after the River Fleet, the street became the nucleus of London's publishing industry when Wynkyn de Worde, William Caxton's assistant, set up a printing press here in 1500. At the same time, Richard Pynson established a publishers and printers next to St Dunstan's Church. Soon other printers and publishers followed, mainly servicing the legal profession. London's first daily newspaper, *The Daily Courant*, was set up here in 1702, in rooms above the White Hart Inn, capitalising on Fleet Street's strategic location between the City of London and Westminster – the two main sources of news. The street was also famous for its taverns (William Shakespeare and Ben Jonson frequented Ye Old Mitre, now at No. 37), and infamous as the location for Sweeney Todd's barbarous barbershop.

Located just off Fleet Street, on Dorset Rise, is **St Bride's**. Famous as the model for the classic tiered wedding cake, St Bride's octagonal spire was added to Wren's 1672 church in 1703. It is the second tallest of Wren's churches at 69 metres (226 feet); only St Paul's has a higher pinnacle. Because of its proximity to Fleet Street, it is the traditional venue for memorial services for journalists, as the wall plaques will attest. St Bride's also had a number of famous parishioners, including Milton, Dryden, and Pepys. The site has been

St Bride's

used as a place of worship since the 7th century – possibly the earliest in London – and may have been set up by Irish monks who named it after St Bridget. The present church is the seventh to stand on the site; the crypt contains remnants of some of the earlier churches as well as a section of Roman pavement.

St Bride's
Opening times: 8am–6pm Mon–Fri, 10am–3.30pm Sat, 10am–6.30pm Sun
www.stbrides.com
Tel: 020-7427 0133

Holborn Viaduct ❼

Return to Fleet Street and turn right, then take a left onto Farringdon Street. The Holborn Viaduct will be ahead of you. This impressive Victorian bridge was built between 1863 and 1869 to improve traffic circulation in this congested part of the city. Designed by the surveyor William Haywood, it features four statues by Henry Bursill: *Commerce* and *Agriculture* on the south side, *Science* and *Fine Arts* on the north. The viaduct is best seen from Farringdon Street, which is linked to it via a staircase.

Turn left from Farringdon Street onto Plumtree Court, and the top of this steep street, you will see **St Andrew**, **Holborn**, one of Wren's largest churches. There has been a church here since the 10th century, and Roman pottery was found during excavations of the crypt in 2001–2002. The church actually survived the Great Fire but was in such a bad state that it eventually had to be demolished. The base part of the tower is original – it was re-clad in marble when the new church was built.

St Andrew, Holborn
Opening times: 9am–5pm Mon–Fri; admission free
www.london.anglican.org/articles/open-church-st-andrew-holborn

Hatton Garden ❽

From Plumtree Court turn left onto Shoe Lane and then take a sharp right onto St Andrew Street; at the roundabout take the second right onto Charterhouse Street and Ely Place will be on your left.

St Ethelreda's Church is at No. 14. Named after an Anglo-Saxon saint and built as part of the Bishop of Ely's palace, this small but delightful chapel dates from around 1250 and is one of the oldest Roman Catholic churches in England. It also has something of a topsy-turvy history. Having been the Spanish ambassador's private chapel in 1620, a time when Catholic services were outlawed in the rest of England, the chapel managed to survive Cromwell's demolition of the rest of the bishop's palace thirty years later. When architect Charles Cole developed Ely Place into an elegant residential enclave in the 1770s, the chapel was refitted in a Georgian style, and then shortly after Catholic Emancipation (1829) it actually became an Anglican place of worship. It was then bought by a Catholic priest in the 1870s who restored it to Catholic use.

Return to Charterhouse Street and turn right, then take the next right and you will be on **Hatton Garden**. This is the centre of London's lucrative diamond trade, and home to a large number of jewellers. The area is also becoming increasingly popular with media and publishing companies. The street takes its name from the gardens of what was originally Ely House and is named for Sir Christopher Hatton, the Elizabethan courtier who leased the palace from the bishops – and then promptly opened a tavern in the crypt.

St Ethelreda's Church
Opening times: 8am–5pm Mon–Sat, 8am–12.30pm Sun; admission free
www.stetheldreda.com
Tel: 020-7405 1061

Gray's Inn ❾

Retrace your steps down Hatton Garden and turn right onto Holborn. The **Staple Inn** will be on your left just after Furnival Street. This was formerly a wool staple – a place where wool was weighed and taxed. It survived the Great Fire only to be wrecked by German bombs during World War II, but has since been substantially restored and looks very much as it might have done at the time of Elizabeth I. Its half-timbered exterior supports a cruck roof and surrounds a courtyard. The interior contains a great hall while the ground-level shops have a more 19th-century feel. The Staple Inn faces straight down Gray's Inn Road.

Walk down this road and **Gray's Inn** will be on your left. The Honourable Society of Gray's Inn, as it is officially known, is the smallest of London's four Inns of Court, and known for its pretty gardens (known as 'Walks'), which have existed since the late 16th century. The legal profession's involvement with this site goes back ever further, to 1370, when law clerks and their

Staple Inn

apprentices began to locate themselves here. The wily Elizabethan lawyer Francis Bacon had chambers here, and at least one of Shakespeare's plays, A *Comedy of Errors*, was premiered in Gray's Inn Hall (in 1594).

Staple Inn
Not open to the public
www.greatlondonlandmarks.com/place/staple-inn

Gray's Inn
www.graysinn.org.uk

> **Did You Know?**
> Charles Dickens worked as a clerk in Gray's Inn in 1827–28.

London Silver Vaults ❿

Return to Holborn and turn right. Then turn left onto Chancery Lane and the **London Silver Vaults** will be on your left at Nos. 53–64. This is one of the most unusual shopping experiences in the country. After going down a staircase and through steel security doors, you will discover a treasure trove of silver specialists selling everything from swizzle sticks to solid-silver armchairs, from classic Georgian silver pieces to cutting-edge modern creations. London silver has been much sought after for centuries, and reached a peak of perfection in the Georgian era. These vaults, originating in the Chancery Lane Safe Deposit Company, have been selling to the public for over 50 years, and now represent the largest collection of silver specialists in the world.

London Silver Vaults
Opening times: 9am–5.30pm Mon–Fri, 9am–1pm Sat; admission free
www.silvervaultslondon.com
Tel: 020-7242 3844

Lincoln's Inn ⓫

Continue down Chancery Lane and turn right onto Old Buildings. Follow this winding street and you will emerge at Lincoln's Inn, one of the four Inns of Court that regulate and educate the legal profession in England and Wales. Dating from the 13th century, Lincoln's Inn was already well-established by the time the Third Earl of Lincoln, for whom it is named, encouraged lawyers to move here. It became a formally organised Inn of Court shortly after the Earl's death in 1311. A number of the buildings date back to the late 15th century, making it one of the best-preserved Inns of Court. The chapel, a late-Gothic building, dates from the early 17th-century. Lincoln's Inn was where Oliver Cromwell and John Donne both studied, as did William Penn, the founder of the American state of Pennsylvania.

Lincoln's Inn Hall

Exit Lincoln's Inn via the Tudor-style archway at the end of New Square and you will be at **Lincoln's Inn Fields**, the largest square in London. This was originally a site for public executions, particularly of religious martyrs under the Tudors and Stuarts. It was laid out in the 1630s as a speculative real-estate development by William Newton, at which time it was the fashionable heart of London. Students at Lincoln's Inn made Newton promise the square would always remain open and today it contains tennis courts as well as numerous pleasant walkways. The land was purchased by London County Council in 1895, and is now the site of a soup kitchen for London's homeless.

Lincoln's Inn
www.lincolnsinn.org.uk
Tel: 020-7405 1393

Lincoln's Inn Chapel
Opening times: 9am–5pm Mon–Fri; admission free

Lincoln's Inn Fields
Opening times: 7am–7pm Mon–Fri; admission free

Holborn

Sir John Soane's Museum ⑫

Located on the north side of Lincoln's Inn Fields is Sir John Soane's Museum. This labyrinthine museum was the home of the 19th-century architect John Soane, who designed the Bank of England, Pitzhanger Manor and the Dulwich Picture Gallery. But it wasn't simply a home; it was also a place where students and amateur enthusiasts of architecture and the arts could come and learn. Merging three Georgian mansions into a single unit, Soane created a mini-museum crammed with artwork, all shown to advantage by his brilliant design innovations: top-lit rooms (a device he also used at the now-demolished Bank of England); a mirrored, domed ceiling for the breakfast room; cleverly placed mirrors to illuminate dark corners; and an ingenious space-saving system of folding panels to hang his countless paintings.

Stylistically the building is a mix of Neoclassicism and Gothic, with the exterior featuring a somewhat starkly designed central projection in Portland stone, while the library's interior is distinctly medieval in feel. For the architectural enthusiast – or indeed anyone who likes antiques or simply the quirkier side of life – this is one museum not to be missed.

Sir John Soane's Museum
Opening times: 10am–5pm Wed–Sun; admission free
www.soane.org
Tel: 020-7405 2107

Old Curiosity Shop ⑬

Leave Lincoln's Inn Fields via Portsmouth Street and the Old Curiosity Shop will be on your left at Nos. 13–14. This funny little building looks indeed as if it could have been used as an illustration for a Dickens novel. It is probably too much of a coincidence to expect it to be the actual model for Dickens's famous work, but it is a genuine 17th-century building and probably the oldest shop in the city. Its timber detailing, projecting upper floor and tiled roof give a hint of what London's streets must have been like in Dickens's time.

Link to Bloomsbury walk: Return to Lincoln's Inn Fields and leave it via Remnant Street. Turn right onto Kingsway and follow it as it turns into Southampton Row.

Bloomsbury

Nearest Tube: Holborn
Approximate walking time: 2 hours 30 minutes

Bloomsbury

Bloomsbury is an elegant district, with wide, straight streets and expansive Georgian squares. The name itself became a byword for intellectual and literary life in London in the first half of the 20th century, centred as it was on the magnificent British Museum and the University of London. Bloomsbury was also home to a number of famous writers, including Virginia Woolf, George Bernard Shaw and William Butler Yeats. Long an important centre in London's book trade, the area has in recent times seen many publishers move out; however there are still some excellent bookshops around. To the north lies St Pancras International, a train station with a fairy-tale Victorian hotel. Next door to it is the popular new British Library, while farther along the road is the elegant Greek Revival St Pancras Parish Church and the Wellcome Collection, which contains a fascinating array of historical medical instruments. Finally, a good spot to relax at the end of this walk is Charlotte Street, with its many excellent restaurants and bars, including the Fitzroy Tavern.

BLOOMSBURY

KING'S CROSS
ST PANCRAS

8 9

EUSTON

10

EUSTON
SQUARE

11

Eversholt St

Euston Rd

Upp Woburn Pl

Tavistock Sq

Euston Rd

Warren
Street

Euston Rd

Fitzroy Sq

12

Gower St

Grafton Way

Whitfield St

Tottenham Court Rd

Whitfield St

Gordon St

Woburn Pl

Tavistock Sq

Huntley St

7

Brunswick Sq

Coram's
Fields

Doughty St

Gray's Inn Rd

Judd St

Grays Inn Rd

RUSSELL
SQUARE

Guilford St

Lamb's Conduit St

Queen Sq

Mortimer St

Goodge St

13

Scala St
Charlotte St

Windmill St

Goodge St

Tottenham Court Rd

Bedford Sq

4

Russell Sq

Montague St

Bloomsbury St

Museum St

3

New Oxford St

Great Russell St

2

Bloomsbury Way

Southampton Row

Kingsway

Holborn

1

Northampton Row

Guilford St

5

6

Queen Sq

Lamb's Conduit St

Start

Holborn

HOLBORN

GOODGE
STREET

0   250m

KEY

1. Bloomsbury Square
2. St George's, Bloomsbury
3. British Museum
4. Russell Square
5. Queen Square
6. Charles Dickens Museum
7. Foundling Museum
8. British Library
9. St Pancras International
10. St Pancras Parish Church
11. Wellcome Collection
12. Fitzroy Square
13. Charlotte Street

Foundling Museum

Bloomsbury

Bloomsbury Square ❶

Leave Holborn station and walk up Southampton Row; **Sicilian Avenue** will be on your left. This charming pedestrian street has a distinctly southern European feel, even if the London weather doesn't always cooperate. Laid out by R.J. Worley in 1910, it was designed as a pedestrian shopping street, with accommodation above the shops. Today it is an unexpected urban treat; the colonnades that close off either end give the street a real sense of enclosure – it's almost as if you're entering another world, even if only for a few moments.

Continue along Sicilian Avenue and turn left onto Bloomsbury Way. **Bloomsbury Square** will be on your right. This is one of the oldest squares in London, laid out in 1661 by the Fourth Earl of Southampton. An imposing mansion used to grace the northern side of the square, but by the end of the 19th century the area was no longer fashionable, at least with the upper classes, so the great house was sold and demolished, replaced by the terrace we see today. A young Benjamin Disraeli lived at No. 6 for a time (his father's house), but as the 20th century wore on, even these middle-class residents moved out, leaving the houses, like those on many a Georgian square, to be turned into offices. The Royal Pharmaceutical Society of Great Britain is housed in an 18th-century building on the south side of the square, which is partly credited to John Nash, while the eastern side of the square is home to the early 20th-century Victoria House, which nearly became London's City Hall in 2000. The square's garden is a pleasant place to stroll.

St George's, Bloomsbury ❷

Continue along Bloomsbury Way, and St George's, Bloomsbury will be on your right. Designed in typically exuberant Baroque style by Nicholas Hawksmoor, this was one of the 50 new churches planned for the new areas of London after 1710. Only about a dozen were built, but Hawksmoor was responsible for six of them. St George's, Bloomsbury is the most complex – and probably the best. The church's site presented unusual challenges in that it ran north to south, making it difficult to place the altar facing east – a liturgical requirement. To solve this, Hawksmoor provided *two* axes for the building: north to south as well as east to west. He then created a large space that seems to sit at the church's centre, lit by clerestory windows. The church's tower when first built was the subject of much derision: the figure of King George I on top, sporting a Roman toga and surrounded by frolicking lions and unicorns, was thought too un-Christian and too heroic. Indeed he does look a little ridiculous.

St George's, Bloomsbury
Opening times: 1.30–3.30pm Wed, 1–3pm Thur, 1.30–3.30 Fri,
noon–1pm Sun
Admission free
www.stgeorgesbloomsbury.org.uk

British Museum ❸

Continue along Bloomsbury Way and turn right onto Museum
Street. The British Museum will be ahead of you, at the end
of the short street that is lined with cafés and bookshops.

Along with the Louvre in Paris, the British Museum is one of the world's
most popular museums. Its collection is suitably magnificent. It is also the
world's oldest public museum, founded in 1753 to house the effects of the
physician Sir Hans Sloane, who helped establish the Chelsea Physic Garden.
Sloane's bequest was augmented by a number of others throughout the
18th century – including George IV's library – all of which were displayed in
nearby Montague House. It was decided to build a custom-made museum in
the early 19th century. The buttoned-down Neoclassicism employed by the
architect Sir Robert Smirke, while lacking the exuberance of a Soane or Dance,
is actually perfectly appropriate for such a monumental public building. In fact
this style, with its minimal ornamental detail lending the building an air of
Greek restraint, became highly influential. Smirke's work was also lauded for
not being too expensive, and for being well built – not the most glamorous
of attributes, perhaps, but important nonetheless.

The museum has been altered and extended many times since being
built in 1823–57. The circular Reading Room now sits in the middle of the
Great Court – formerly an open-air courtyard but now roofed over by a high-
tech glass canopy.

The museum's collection spans two million years, covering every major
civilisation, with 94 galleries stretching over 4 kilometres (2.5 miles). The
collection's highlights include the Parthenon Sculptures, formerly known as the
Elgin Marbles, which were brought to England from the Parthenon in Athens

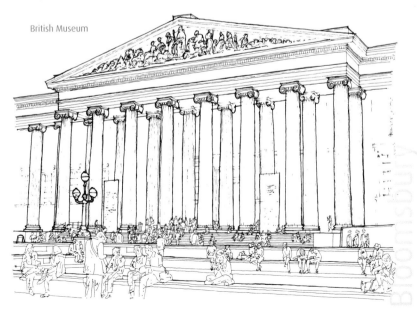

British Museum

by Lord Elgin, and sold to the British government in 1816; the Rosetta Stone, which enabled Jean-Francois Champollion to decipher Egyptian hieroglyphs for the first time; and the remarkable Sutton Hoo hoard – the contents of a 7th-century Anglo-Saxon royal burial ship found in 1939.

British Museum
Opening times: 10am–5.30pm daily; admission free
www.britishmuseum.org
Tel: 0800-218 2222

Russell Square ❹

Leave the British Museum by turning left onto Great Russell Street, then left again onto Montague Street, and you will come to Russell Square. Most of the streets and squares in this part of London take their names from the Russell family – the Dukes of Bedford – including of course Bedford, Tavistock (the Marquess Tavistock is the courtesy title of the Duke's eldest son) and Woburn (after their country house, Woburn Abbey, in Bedfordshire). The dukes developed their land into this elegant residential enclave in the 17th and 18th centuries, with Russell Square being formed out of the original gardens of Bedford House (now demolished). Most of these once-gracious homes are now offices. The square was re-landscaped in 2002 based on the original early 19th-century layout by Humphrey Repton, and contains a fountain, a café and a statue of the Fifth Duke, who is shown with sheep and a plough (he was a keen farmer).

Charles Fitzroy Doll's magnificent **Russell Hotel** was opened in 1900 and takes up the northern half of the square's eastern side. A riot of balconies, bay windows and turrets, it is one of the few Edwardian-era grand hotels left in the city. The western side of the square is home to the University of London. A blue plaque commemorates the place where T.S. Eliot used to work as a lowly poetry editor for a publishing house while writing some of the 20th century's most sublime verse. Beyond this towers the magnificent Senate House of the University of London. Designed by Charles Holden in the Art Deco style and built in 1932–37, it was used as the Ministry of Information during the war and was the model for George Orwell's Ministry of Truth in *Nineteen Eighty-Four*. It contains a wonderful library.

Queen Square ❺

Leave Russell Square via Guilford Street and take the next right-hand turn, which leads through a small side street onto the long, narrow Queen Square. Originally called Queen Anne's Square, it now houses a statue of Queen Charlotte, wife of George III. It was in a house on this square that the King was treated, unsuccessfully, for the hereditary disease that drove him mad. The narrow north side of the square was originally left open so that the residents could enjoy views north to Hampstead and Highgate. Today it is almost completely surrounded by grim-looking hospital buildings, although some charming early Georgian buildings remain on the square's west side.

Charles Dickens Museum ⑥

Return to Guilford Street and turn right. Walk as far as Doughty Street and turn right again. The Charles Dickens Museum will be on your left at No. 48. This is where the famous novelist lived from 1837 to 1839. Although he also lived in a number of other London homes, this is the only one that has survived. The three years or so that he spent here were among the most productive of his life: he produced *Oliver Twist* and *Nicholas Nickleby*, began *Barnaby Rudge* and completed the *Pickwick Papers*. Dickens's increasing success meant that he was soon able to move out of this pleasant but modest terraced house and into a series of ever grander homes.

This building was almost demolished in 1923 but was fortunately saved by the Dickens Fellowship. It was then renovated and the museum opened in 1925. Spread over four floors, it contains the world's most important collection of paintings, rare editions, manuscripts and furniture relating to Dickens's life and work.

Charles Dickens Museum
Opening times: 10am–5pm Mon–Sat (Jan–Nov); 10am–5pm daily (Dec)
Admission charges
www.dickensmuseum.com
Tel: 020-7405 2127

Foundling Museum ⑦

Retrace your steps down Guilford Street, and **Coram's Fields** will be on your right. This is one of London's largest playgrounds, and extremely popular with children. Its is named after Thomas Coram, a retired ship's captain, who founded a refuge for abandoned children in 1722 after being horrified by the sight of so much poverty on the streets of London when he returned from working in the Americas. Dogs are not allowed, and all adults must be accompanied by children.

To the north of Coram's Fields, the **Foundling Museum** sits at No. 40 Brunswick Square. In 1739 a Foundling Hospital was established after a successful petition to George II. To help raise funds, Coram called on his friend, William Hogarth, to donate some of his paintings to the hospital. Wealthy art-lovers were then encouraged to view the paintings and give generously when they saw the good work being done for the hospital's children. The original hospital was located on Lamb's Conduit Street and was demolished in the 1920s. Two lovely 18th-century interiors were rescued and are now located in the museum. The ground floor shows the story of how thousands of children were cared for by the hospital, while the impressive collection of 18th-century painting, sculpture and furniture is displayed on the first floor.

Foundling Museum
Opening times: 10am–5pm Tue–Sat; 11am–5pm Sun
Admission charges
www.foundlingmuseum.org.uk
Tel: 020-7842 3600

British Library ⑧

Leave Coram's Fields by turning right onto Hunter Street. Follow it to the end as it turns into Judd Street and comes out onto Euston Road. The British Library will be across the road.

This red-brick building by Sir Colin St John Wilson, opened in 1997 after nearly 20 years of construction, houses the nation's collection of books, manuscripts, newspapers and magazines, maps, stamps, music recordings and videos. A copy of almost every printed book in the United Kingdom is held here – there are more than 16 million. Though primarily a research library, there are exhibition galleries open to the public. Some of the library's prize possessions include two Gutenberg Bibles, two copies of the Magna Carta, one of Leonardo da Vinci's notebooks and the Lindisfarne Gospels.

The building was controversial, as any grand new public building will be. The fact that it did not make any attempt to look as if it had been built two or three hundred years earlier upset more than a few people, some of them very influential indeed, but it is in fact quite a fine essay in late 20th-century civic architecture.

British Library
Opening times: 9.30am–8pm Mon–Thur, 9.30am–6pm Fri, 9.30am–5pm Sat, 11am–5pm Sun; admission free
www.bl.uk
Tel: 0330-333 1144

St Pancras International ⑨

Located next door to the British Library is St Pancras International. This railway station is where the Eurostar departs for mainland Europe via the Channel Tunnel, and is the most spectacular of the three rail termini along Euston Road. The extravagant red-brick-and-stone Gothic fantasy that sits alongside it is not actually part of the station; it was built between 1868 and 1874 as the Midland Grand Hotel by Sir George Gilbert Scott. Even the architect himself thought he had probably overdone it somewhat for what was basically a railway hotel – he might have been compensating himself for having been forced by the prime minister Lord Palmerston to design the Foreign Office in

St Pancras International

an Italian Renaissance style. When it was threatened with demolition in the early 20th century, the poet John Betjeman campaigned successfully to save it – and there is today a statue of him on the upper level. Used as an office building from 1935 to the early 1980s, it has recently been lavishly restored and lends a fairy-tale air to an otherwise grim and busy street.

St Pancras International
www.stpancras.com

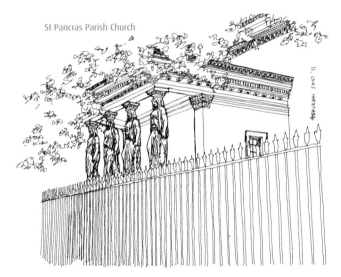

St Pancras Parish Church

St Pancras Parish Church ⑩

Leave St Pancras International and turn right onto Euston Road. St Pancras Parish Church will be on your left, overlooking the corner of Upper Woburn Place. Named after a Roman martyr, it is also known as St Pancras New Church, to differentiate it from St Pancras Old Church on Pancras Road. This elegant Greek Revival church was designed by William Inwood and his son Henry in 1822, based on the Erechtheum at the Acropolis in Athens, famous for its caryatids (columns in the form of women, supporting the roof with their heads). The interior consists of a simple, galleried space, the length of which conveys a sense of drama very much in keeping with the rest of the style. The Greek detailing extends to the wooden pulpit, which stands on miniature Ionic columns. The warren of corridors in the crypt is used for temporary art exhibitions.

Located just behind the church is **Woburn Walk**, a well-restored street of bow-fronted shops designed by Thomas Cubitt in 1822. The high pavement on the east side of the street protected the shops from mud thrown up by carriages ploughing their way through the poorly paved streets in the 19th century. The poet William Butler Yeats lived at No. 5 from 1895 to 1919.

St Pancras Parish Church
Opening times: 8am–6pm Mon– Thur; 7.30–11.30am and 5.30–7pm Sun
www.stpancraschurch.org
Tel: 020-7388 1461

Wellcome Collection ⑪

Continue along Euston Road and the Wellcome Collection will be on your left. This is named after Sir Henry Wellcome, the eminent pharmacist and collector of books, paintings and objects relating to the history of medicine. The

Wellcome Building is dedicated to this wondrous collection. The impressive symmetrical Neoclassical block dressed in Portland stone features a centrally placed portico of four Ionic columns. Inside there are three exhibition spaces, an auditorium, an events space, a café and bookshop, as well as the Wellcome Library – the largest library in the world dedicated to the history of medicine. Some of the exhibits are unusual, like a used guillotine blade, or Napoleon's toothbrush; others are simply bizarre, but they reflect what was thought of as cutting-edge medical practice at the time.

Wellcome Collection
Opening times: 10am–6pm Tue, Wed, Fri–Sun, 10am–8pm Thur; admission free
www.wellcomecollection.org
Tel: 020-7611 2222

Fitzroy Square ⑫

Continue along Euston Road, take a left onto Gower Street, then turn right onto Grafton Way, and you will come to Fitzroy Square, one of the loveliest of London's squares. The fine buildings that grace this square were speculative developments by the First Baron Southampton, begun in 1794. The terraces on the eastern and western sides – designed by Robert Adam and completed by his brothers James and William – were meant to form unified wholes, finished uniformly in Portland stone; as a result, the terraces look more like palaces than rows of individual houses. The northern and western sides of the square took decades to finish; these are finished in a cheaper stucco and lack the grace of the other sides. Many writers have been residents here, including George Bernard Shaw, Virginia Woolf and Ford Madox Brown. Ian McEwan used to live at No. 11 and even set one of his novels here (*Saturday*).

Fitzroy Square

Charlotte Street ⑬

Leave Fitzroy Square via Fitzroy Street and it will turn into Charlotte Street after a short distance. Somewhat overshadowed by the 189-metre (620-foot) **BT Tower** to the north, this street is surprisingly vibrant for a part of London that is not particularly noted for its nightlife. Full of good restaurants and bars, it is also home to small artisan workshops and clothing shops that service the larger clothes and furniture shops of nearby Oxford Street and Tottenham Court Road. John Constable lived and worked here, at No. 76.

Located just off Charlotte Street, on the corner of Scala Street and Whitfield Street, is **Pollock's Toy Museum**. Benjamin Pollock was renowned for his toy theatres in the late 19th and early 20th centuries. This museum, which is a paradise for children, originally opened in Monmouth Street, Covent Garden, in 1956 before moving here in 1969. Laid out with children in mind, it ranges across two almost perfectly intact 18th-century houses. The small rooms are crammed with historic toys from all over the world, including dolls and puppets, trains and cars, rocking horses and doll's houses. The last room is devoted to the stages and puppets from Pollock's original theatres, and also contains a reconstruction of his workshop. The museum has an enticing toyshop, again delightful for children – perhaps slightly less so for parents.

Leave Scala Street by turning left onto Charlotte Street, and the **Fitzroy Tavern** will be on your left just before the corner of Windmill Street. This traditional English pub was the centre of London's literary life between the world wars, leading Dylan Thomas to dub the entire area 'Fitzrovia'. A Writers and Artists Bar in the basement shows pictures of former customers, including Thomas himself, as well as George Orwell and the painter Augustus John.

BT Tower
Not open to the public except during Open House weekend in September

Pollock's Toy Museum
Opening times: 10am–5pm Mon–Sat; admission charges
www.pollockstoys.com
Tel: 020-7636 3452

Link to Regent's Park walk: Leave Charlotte Street by turning left onto Goodge Street. Follow it as it turns into Mortimer Street and you will come to Langham Place on your right.

Pollock's Toy Museum

Regent's Park

Nearest Tube: Oxford Circus
Approximate walking time: 3 hours

Regent's Park

In the early years of the 19th century, Regent's Park was linked to the Prince Regent's home – Carlton House, Pall Mall – via Portland Place and the new Regent Street. Fashionable since it was first laid out, this beautiful green space is lined with elegant white Neoclassical terraces, and also contains London Zoo, a bucolic stretch of Regent's Canal, and London's main mosque. To the south lies Marylebone, once a medieval village and now home to London's highest concentration of Georgian houses. Farther south lies Oxford Street, one of the world's busiest shopping thoroughfares. This walk takes in some of London's most popular tourist attractions, including Madame Tussauds waxworks and the Sherlock Holmes Museum.

REGENT'S PARK

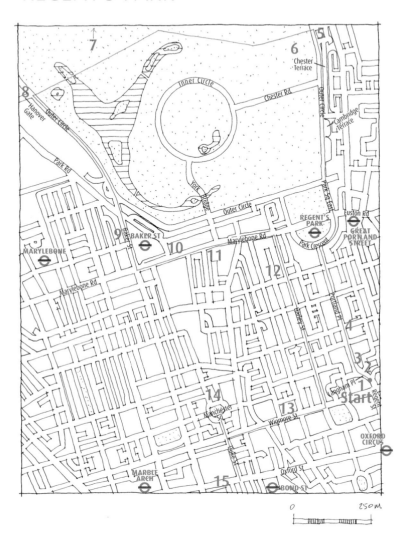

KEY

All Souls

Regent's Park

Langham Hotel ❶

Leave Oxford Circus station and walk up Regent Street until you come to Langham Place. The Langham Hotel will be on your left at No. 1. This imposing Victorian hotel, while not particularly architecturally distinguished, was one of the city's grandest places to stay when it opened in 1865. Guests included Oscar Wilde, Mark Twain and Antonin Dvorak. But like many 19th-century grand hotels, it fell out of fashion in the 20th and into disuse – at least as a hotel. The BBC used it for a number of years as their recording studios and record library. Recently restored to its gaudy Victorian glory, it has once again become a popular place to stay for those who don't have to worry too much about money.

All Souls ❷

Facing the Langham Hotel across Langham Place is All Souls. Designed in 1824 by John Nash, this is the only one of his churches still around. Its round portico acts as the turning point linking Regent Street – which Nash built to link the Prince Regent's palace in Pall Mall – to the newly laid-out Regent's Park in the north. The columns of the main portico are essentially Ionic, but have been altered to feature angels' wings instead of the usual scrolls – a foreshadowing of the Victorian love of bending the rules of Neoclassicism to suit extravagant tastes. Given its location next door to BBC's Broadcasting House, the church has had close ties to that organisation. Church services used to be broadcast from here daily.

All Souls
Opening times: 10am–5pm Mon–Fri, 9am–2pm and 5–7.30pm Sun
www.allsouls.org
Tel: 020-7580 3522

Broadcasting House ❸

Across the road from All Souls is Broadcasting House (you can see an illustration of it in the Architectural Styles chapter). Officially opened in 1932, it was designed in an elegantly monumental Art Deco style by the architect George Val Myer in collaboration with the BBC's civil engineer, Marmaduke Tudsbery Tudsbery. The BBC moved to newer studios in Shepherd's Bush in the 1960s, and this building was kept as a home for management offices and as a recording studio for BBC Radio 3 and 4. The building's impressive stone front, which curves elegantly along the street, is dominated by a bas-relief by Eric Gill. Originally intended to represent God and Man, it was considered too religious for public taste, so the figures became the characters Prospero and Ariel from Shakespeare's *Tempest* instead. Since Ariel is supposed to be a spirit of the air, this was thought an ideal personification of the new medium of television. The interiors were originally the work of Australian-Irish architect Raymond McGrath – all executed in a smooth Art Deco style. The building was cleverly extended in 2013. New Broadcasting House consists of a large new wing that wraps itself around Langham Street to create a narrow but pleasant piazza at its entrance, which has All Souls as a focal point.

Portland Place ④

Return to Langham Place and turn right and you will come to Portland Place. Robert and James Adam laid out this wide street for the Duke of Portland in 1773. At that time Langham Place was taken up by the large town house of Lord Foley, who insisted that his view to the north not be restricted by the new street. Portland Place, at 33 metres (110 feet), is indeed unusually wide for central London. The street has some magnificent Georgian houses, many of them home to embassies or professional associations. Nos. 27 to 47, on the west (south of Devonshire Street), are all original, while at No. 66 is the Royal Institute of British Architects. Designed by Grey Wornum in 1934 in a severe Art Deco style, it is adorned with symbolic bas-reliefs and statues; the bronze front doors depict London buildings and the River Thames. Portland Place opens out into **Park Crescent** at its north end. Facing Regent's Park, this breathtaking semi-circular sweep of white stuccoed facades, with twinned Ionic columns supporting

Park Crescent

BROCKEN JAN '11

Regent's Park

continuous balconies across the house fronts, forms a magnificent urban space. Seemingly well-preserved, the western terrace was actually rebuilt as an office block in the 1960s – only its façade was retained. The Crescent acts as the suitably impressive northern end of Nash's great ceremonial route through central London, from St James's Park to Regent's Park.

Cumberland Terrace ❺

From Park Crescent walk along Park Square East until you come to Outer Circle. Follow this and you will come to Cumberland Terrace after passing a number of other attractive terraces, including Cambridge and Chester. Cumberland Terrace was designed to stand facing the new palace (unbuilt) that John Nash was designing for the Prince Regent in Regent's Park. Completed in 1826, Cumberland Terrace was the longest and most elaborate of the terraces surrounding the park, with three main blocks linked by decorative arches. The central block consists of a large pediment above a long Ionic colonnade. Originally made of 31 houses, it is still in residential use, although some of the houses have been converted into flats. This is one of the treasures of the city's architecture, effortlessly combining early 19th-century elegance with an understanding of London's impressive urban scale.

Regent's Park ❻

Enter Regent's Park via Cumberland Gate. This beautiful 166-hectare (410-acre) park was once part of the Manor of Tyburn owned by Barking Abbey. When Henry VIII dissolved the monasteries in 1536 he turned it into a royal park. Commissioned by the Prince Regent to create a master plan for the park and surrounding area in 1811, John Nash designed what was to be in effect a precursor of the garden suburb, except with a royal palace surrounded by imposing villas dotted across the picturesque landscape, in turn surrounded by elegant Neoclassical terraces. These would all be linked to the Prince's palace at Pall Mall via the grand new Regent Street and stately Portland Place – which Nash capped off with the graceful curve of Park Crescent. The Prince was delighted, thinking it a scheme to rival anything Napoleon was planning in Paris. The great streets and terraces were built, and they were indeed magnificent, but the palace never materialised.

Today, the Outer Circle is lined with Nash's great terraces, while the Inner Circle is centred on the most carefully tended part of the park, Queen Mary's Gardens, and also contains an **Open-Air Theatre**, best known for staging Shakespeare's plays in the summer. Regent's Park also contains a number of formal gardens, rolling parkland, a lake, sporting facilities, and in the northern part, **London Zoo**. Founded in 1828, this is the oldest zoo in the world and one of London's main tourist attractions.

Regent's Park
Opening times: 5am–9pm daily; admission free

Open-Air Theatre
Opening times: Summer months
www.openairtheatre.org
Tel: 0333-400 3562

London Zoo
Opening times: 10am–6pm (varies according to season); admission charges
www.zsl.org/zsl-london-zoo
Tel: 020-7449 6200

Regent's Canal

Running along the northern border of Regent's Park is Regent's Canal. This was opened in 1820 to link the Grand Union Canal in Paddington to the London Docks. John Nash was initially very enthusiastic about it; he even wanted it to run through the heart of the park. He was persuaded, however, that the bad language of the boatmen would be offensive to the park's genteel residents. This was lucky for the park because as soon as steam power took over from cart horses the barges got larger and dirtier, and more dangerous – a barge carrying gunpowder blew up near London Zoo in 1874, killing the crew and a number of animals. Competition from the railways eventually saw the canal fall into decline, but it has recently been upgraded, and makes for a pleasant stroll, or a boat trip from Paddington's Little Venice to Camden Lock, which has a lively craft market.

Regent's Canal
www.canalrivertrust.org.uk/enjoy-the-waterways/canal-and-river-network/regents-canal

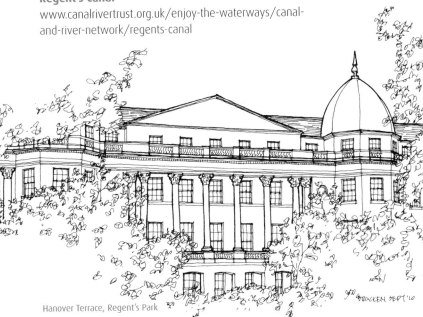

Hanover Terrace, Regent's Park

London Central Mosque

London Central Mosque ⑧

Leave Regent's Park via Hanover Gate and the London Central Mosque will be straight ahead of you at No. 146 Park Ride. Also known as the Islamic Cultural Centre or Regent's Park Mosque, this was built in 1974–1977 to cater for the increasing number of Muslims in London. Sir Frederick Gibberd's design is made up of a main building – consisting of two prayer halls topped by a massive golden dome – and three-story wings that house the entrance hall, library, reading room, administration offices as well as a minaret. The main prayer hall, fitted out with an impressive chandelier and a vast carpet, holds up to five thousand worshippers. The complex is also home to a small bookshop and halal café. Remember to dress appropriately and remove your shoes when going inside.

London Central Mosque
Opening times: 10.30am–4pm Mon–Thur; admission charges
www.iccuk.org
Tel: 020-7725 2152

> **Did You Know?**
> The land for the London Central Mosque was donated by King George VI in return for a site for an Anglican cathedral in Cairo.

Sherlock Holmes Museum ⑨

With Regent's Park on your left, walk along Outer Circle until you come to Baker Street. The Sherlock Holmes Museum will be on your right. Opened in 1990, the museum received special permission from the City of Westminster to carry the address 221b Baker Street – even though no such address ever existed – as that is where the fictional sleuth is supposed to have lived (the house in fact sits between Nos. 237 and 241). This Georgian town house, dating from 1815, was for a time a boarding house, much like the one that Holmes and Watson inhabited during their adventures. It has been decorated to resemble the flat from the stories, and visitors are greeted by Holmes's 'housekeeper' Mrs Hudson before being shown around. The gift shop sells the Holmes stories as well as the detective's signature deerstalker hat.

Sherlock Holmes Museum
Opening times:
9.30am–6pm daily
Admission charges
www.sherlock-holmes.co.uk
Tel: 020-7224 3688

Sherlock Holmes Museum

Madame Tussauds ⑩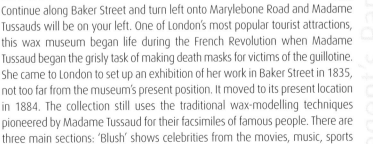

Continue along Baker Street and turn left onto Marylebone Road and Madame Tussauds will be on your left. One of London's most popular tourist attractions, this wax museum began life during the French Revolution when Madame Tussaud began the grisly task of making death masks for victims of the guillotine. She came to London to set up an exhibition of her work in Baker Street in 1835, not too far from the museum's present position. It moved to its present location in 1884. The collection still uses the traditional wax-modelling techniques pioneered by Madame Tussaud for their facsimiles of famous people. There are three main sections: 'Blush' shows celebrities from the movies, music, sports and politics; the 'Chamber of Horrors' features re-creations of the crimes of

Regent's Park

infamous characters such as Dr Crippen, Jack the Ripper and Vlad the Impaler (the model for Bram Stoker's Dracula); and in 'The Spirit of London', historical events such as the Great Fire of 1666 are brought to life.

Madame Tussauds
Opening times: 9am–5pm Tue–Thur, 9am–6pm Fri–Mon; admission charges
www.madametussauds.com/london
Tel: 020-522 1010

St Marylebone Parish Church ⓫

Continue along Marylebone Road, and St Marylebone Parish Church will be on your right. The name Marylebone comes from a 1440 church that was dedicated to St Mary the Virgin and located alongside the Ty stream, or bourne, which used to run from Regent's Park into the Thames; the church thus became known as St Mary le burn, eventually St Marylebone. As London developed, the church became too small for its congregation, and plans were made to build a new one. Even though these plans began in 1770, it wasn't until 1813 that the foundation stone of Thomas Hardwicke's new Neoclassical building was laid, and 1817 before it was completed. Charles Dickens baptised a son in this church and Elizabeth Barrett and Robert Browning were married here in 1846. The interior was overhauled in a mix of Neoclassical and Pre-Raphaelite styles in the 1880s.

St Marylebone Parish Church
Opening times: 9am–5pm Mon–Fri, 8am–4pm Sat and Sun; admission free
www.stmarylebone.org

Harley Street ⓬

Continue along Marylebone Road until you come to Harley Street. Named for the family of the man who developed this part of London, the Earl of Oxford, Harley Street is London's pre-eminent medical enclave. The large, late 18th-century houses were popular with professionals, particularly doctors; today most have been converted into consulting rooms for the highly paid specialists who can afford the rents (many of them still charge in guineas), and the street retains its hushed air of high-class medical efficiency.

Wigmore Hall ⓭

Walk to the end of Harley Street and turn right onto Wigmore Street. Wigmore Hall, with its distinctive glass entrance canopy, will be on your right at No. 36. This is the leading venue for chamber music in London. Designed in 1900 by Thomas Edward Collcutt, architect of the Savoy Hotel, the auditorium contains a near-perfect acoustic and immediately became a firm favourite with performing artists. The building is in a Renaissance style, with the auditorium's interior being decorated with alabaster and marble, with a shallow dome depicting the Soul of Music.

Across the road is the Art Nouveau **Debenham and Freebody's**, a former department store which was founded as a drapers in 1778 and shortened its name to Debenham's when it moved around the corner to Oxford Street in the 1970s.

Wigmore Hall
www.wigmore-hall.org.uk
Tel: 020-7935 2141

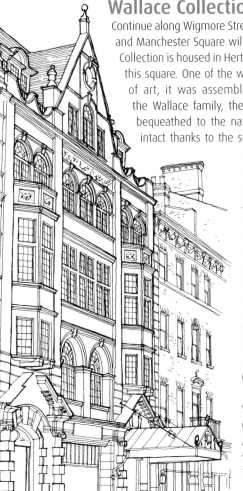

Wallace Collection ⑭

Continue along Wigmore Street, turn right onto Duke Street, and Manchester Square will be ahead of you. The Wallace Collection is housed in Hertford House on the north side of this square. One of the world's finest private collections of art, it was assembled over five generations by the Wallace family, the Marquesses of Hertford, and bequeathed to the nation in 1897. It has remained intact thanks to the stipulation that it should go on permanent display with nothing added or removed. Four new galleries were opened in June 2000 so that more of the collection could be seen. Among its highlights are Frans Hals's *Laughing Cavalier*, Titian's *Perseus and Andromeda* and Rembrandt's *Titus*. There are also portraits by Reynolds, Gainsborough and Romney. Other gems include some Sèvres porcelain and the largest collection of European and Oriental armour in the country.

Wallace Collection
Opening times: 10am–5pm
Admission free
www.wallacecollection.org
Tel: 020-7563 9500

Wigmore Hall

Wallace Collection

Oxford Street ⑮

Leave Manchester Square by going back down Duke Street, and follow it to the end until you come to Oxford Street. This was an old Roman road linking Hampshire with Colchester (the Roman capital). The Earl of Oxford bought the land surrounding the road in the 18th century, and developed it into a residential district, renaming the street after himself in the process. It became popular for entertainment, with theatres, taverns and bear-baiting. It then turned into a popular shopping street in the 19th century, and today, with more than 500 shops along its 2.5-km (1.5-mile) length, it is one of the world's most important retail areas. Some of its renowned department stores include John Lewis Partnership, House of Fraser, and Debenham's.

Perhaps the most famous of them all, though, is **Selfridges**, at No. 400, the second largest department store in the country and a mainstay of Oxford Street since it first opened its doors in 1909. Its founder, the innovative American shopping magnate Harry Gordon Selfridge, tried to make the experience of shopping fun, instead of the chore it was at the end of the 19th century. He laid out merchandise so that the customers could examine it for themselves; he was also the first to think of putting perfume counters on the ground floor, near the entrances – all clever ideas that have since been copied everywhere. The London store, designed by Daniel Burnham, is the chain's flagship.

Link to Kensington walk: Follow Oxford Street westwards until you come to Hyde Park.

Kensington

Nearest Tube: Marble Arch
Approximate walking time: 3 hours

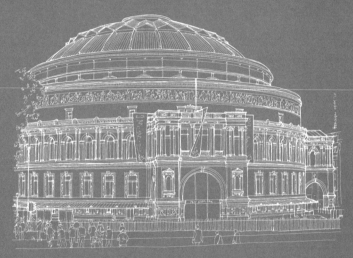

Kensington

Centred on the vast green expanse of Hyde Park – which incorporates Kensington Gardens – this is one of the smartest residential districts in the world. The eastern edge of the park is overlooked by Park Lane (the western edge of Mayfair), while the south is home to Knightsbridge and the legendary Harrods department store. Kensington began life as a small country village and was really only developed in the mid-19th century, when it became a sought-after residential area, particularly for artists. Today it is home to a number of important museums and educational establishments, including the Natural History Museum, the Science Museum, the massive Victoria and Albert Museum, as well as the Royal Colleges of Music and Art. The area also takes in one of London's most popular concert halls, the Royal Albert Hall – venue for the world-famous Proms concerts every summer – and Kensington Palace, home to a number of members of the Royal Family. It also has a more down-to-earth side, with Bayswater and Notting Hill to the north. Notting Hill is home to the famous Portobello Road street market and an annual Caribbean-style street carnival.

KENSINGTON

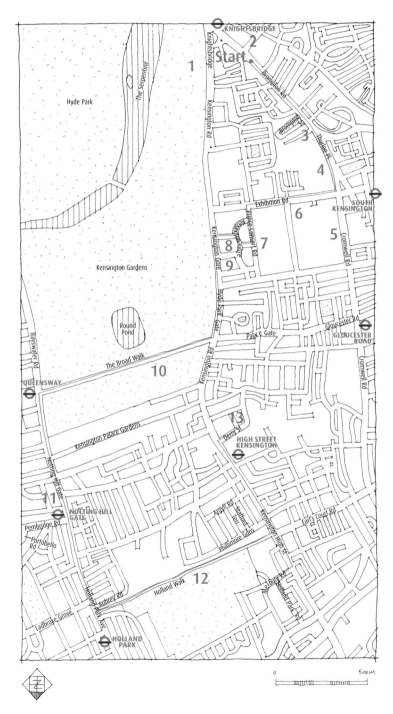

KNIGHTSBRIDGE

Start.

2

1

The Serpentine

Knightsbridge

Hyde Park

Kensington Rd

Brompton Rd

Brompton

3

Thurloe Rd

4

Exhibition Rd

6

SOUTH
KENSINGTON

Prince Consort Rd

Exhibition Rd

5

Cromwell Rd

7

8

Kensington Gardens

Kensington Gore

9

Kensington Gardens

Round
Pond

Hyde Park Gate

Palace Gate

Gloucester Rd

GLOUCESTER
ROAD

Bayswater Rd

The Broad Walk

10

Kensington Rd

Kensington Church St

Cromwell Rd

QUEENSWAY

Kensington Palace Gardens

13

Derry St

HIGH STREET
KENSINGTON

Notting Hill Gate

11

NOTTING HILL
GATE

Pembridge Rd

Argyll Rd

Phillimore Gdns

Earl's Court Rd

Kensington High St

Portobello
Rd

Holland Walk

12

Melbury Rd

Ladbroke Grove

Holland Park Ave

Aubrey Rd

HOLLAND
PARK

Abbotsbury Rd

N

0   500 M

KEY

Kensington

Hyde Park ❶

Leave Marble Arch station and you will be at John Nash's **Marble Arch**. This triumphal arch was designed in 1827 to be the main entrance to Buckingham Palace, but soon proved too narrow for the large coaches and was moved here in 1851. It now stands near what used to be the Tyburn gallows (which are marked by a plaque), where London's most notorious criminals were hanged – a hugely popular spectacle in its day. Only senior members of the royal family and one particular royal artillery regiment are allowed to pass under the arch.

Beside Marble Arch is **Speakers' Corner**. When Britain passed a law in 1872 making it legal to address a crowd on whatever topic a speaker chose, this corner of Hyde Park become the venue of choice for those with a proselytising zeal. It still attracts its fair share of soapbox orators, as well as a few oddballs. Sunday is the best time to catch them in action; the crowds tend to be larger and the heckling more colourful.

Hyde Park has been a royal park since Henry VIII dissolved the monasteries in 1536. Before that it had been a manor owned by Westminster Abbey. Henry used it for hunting but James I opened it to the public, and it has remained one of the city's most popular parks ever since. The Great Exhibition was held here in 1851. This was housed in Joseph Paxton's massive Crystal Palace, which moved to Sydenham after the Exhibition ended, where sadly it burned down in 1936. The Serpentine, an artificial boating lake that divides Hyde Park from Kensington Gardens, was created in 1730 for Queen Caroline, wife of George II. It was formed by damming the Westbourne River.

The **Serpentine Gallery**, in the southeast corner of Kensington Gardens, houses temporary exhibitions of contemporary art. These sometimes spill out into the park. The gallery commissions a different architect every summer to build a pavilion near its café, these are sometimes bizarre and often beautiful.

Hyde Park
Opening times: 5am–midnight daily
www.royalparks.org.uk/parks/hyde-park
Tel: 0300-061 2000

Serpentine Gallery
Opening times: 10am–6pm Tue–Sun; admission free
www.serpentinegalleries.org
Tel: 020-7402 6075

Harrods ❷

Wander Hyde Park at leisure and then exit onto Knightsbridge and turn right. Then take a left onto Brompton Road and Harrods will be on your left. This vast Victorian edifice is without a doubt the world's most famous department

store. Harrods began life in 1824 when Charles Henry Harrod opened a small drapers on Borough High Street in Southwark. He moved to Clerkenwell in 1832 and turned it into a grocers. Two years later he added a shop specialising in tea in Stepney. In order to escape the overcrowded East End, and to capitalise on the crowds flooding into Hyde Park for the Great Exhibition, Harrod took over a small shop on the corner of the store's present site. It consisted of a single room. He employed two shop assistants and a messenger boy. It was his son, Charles Digby Harrod, who really turned the business into the massive emporium it is today. By 1880 he had acquired the adjoining buildings and was employing a staff of more than one hundred. The store burned down in 1883, to be replaced by this massive structure soon afterwards. With its motto of *Omnia Omnibus Ubique* (All Things for All People, Everywhere), the store is famous for being able to provide whatever a customer wants – no matter how bizarre or exotic.

Harrods
www.harrods.com/en-gb
Tel: 020-7730 1234

Harrods

> **Did You Know?**
> Harrods launched the world's first escalator in 1898. Consisting of a woven leather conveyor belt with a mahogany, silver and plate-glass balustrade, it caused a sensation. Customers who made it to the top were offered a glass of brandy to help them recover from their ordeal.

Brompton Oratory ❸

Continue along Brompton Road and the Brompton Oratory will be on your right. This imposing Roman Catholic church was built during a wave of Catholic revival that swept through England in the second half of the 19th century. At 61 metres (200 feet) tall it was the tallest and largest Catholic church in London before Westminster Cathedral opened in 1903. The exterior is faced in Portland stone, while the vaults and dome are made of concrete. The interior makes lavish use of marble as well as metal, plaster and wood-carvings. Some of the treasures have come from churches abroad: Giuseppe Mazzuoli's 17th-century *Twelve Apostles* came from Siena Cathedral in 1895, while the beautiful sculptures on the Lady Altar were created by Tommaso Rues for a Dominican church in Brescia in the 17th century. This mix of artworks from different periods and styles means that the church's interior exhibits a taste that is more than usually catholic – in every sense of the word. The Oratory is also famous for its sung masses.

Brompton Square, which neighbours the Oratory, is a delightful residential enclave off this busy main road.

Brompton Oratory
www.bromptonoratory.co.uk
Tel: 020-7808 0900

Victoria and Albert Museum ❹

Next door to the Brompton Oratory on Thurloe Place sits the Victoria and Albert Museum, popularly known as the V&A. First opened in 1852 at Marlborough House, the current museum houses more than 150 different galleries featuring one of the world's most comprehensive collections of art and design. Highlights of the collection include a series of medieval tapestries known as the Devonshire Hunts, the Music Room from Norfolk House, and Sir George Gilbert Scott's Hereford Screen.

Level 1 houses the China, Japan and South Asian galleries, the Jameel Gallery of Islamic Art, and the textiles and fashion gallery. The British galleries are on Levels 2 and 4 and exhibit British design and decorative art from 1500 to 1900. Level 3 houses the 20th-century galleries as well as the metalwork galleries – the silver collection is particularly fine. Level 4 contains glass, while ceramics are on Level 6. The architecture gallery features drawings, models and architectural fragments from around the world.

Victoria and Albert Museum

Don't miss the museum's cafe, which was originally designed by a then unknown William Morris. The building itself was designed by Aston Webb, in an unoffensive Edwardian mix of stylistic references that don't quite get pulled together despite the wedding-cake cupola topping things off.

Victoria and Albert Museum
Opening times: 10am–5.45pm Sat–Thur, 10am–10pm Fri; admission free
www.vam.ac.uk
Tel: 020-7942 2000

Natural History Museum ❺

Next door to the Victoria and Albert Museum, where Thurloe Place turns into Cromwell Road, is the Natural History Museum. The museum covers the fields of botany, entomology, mineralogy, palaeontology and zoology, and is well-known in particular for its dinosaur skeletons – including a 26-metre (85-foot) diplodocus. A number of the collections have significant historical value as well, for example the specimens collected by Charles Darwin. The museum started out as part of the British Museum but as the collections grew it was decided that a separate building was needed.

Work on this fanciful German Romanesque landmark began in 1873 and the museum opened in 1881. For reasons of economy, the museum was supposed to be built in two stages, but the second stage (consisting of side wings and a rear portion) was never built. Despite the tight budget Waterhouse managed to produce a large and beautifully decorated structure. Terracotta tiles were chosen as a cladding because of the anticipated effects of Victorian London's sooty air. The tiles feature bas-reliefs of flora and fauna – living species on the west wing, and extinct ones on the east. The cathedral-like proportions of the building are naturally lit – gas lighting being considered too dangerous as many of the specimens were preserved in spirits. The museum's romantic skyline has a more mundane side in that it hides the building's water tanks, while the grounds are a popular spot for picnic lunches among office workers from the neighbourhood.

Natural History Museum
Opening times: 10am–5.50pm daily
Admission free
www.nhm.ac.uk
Tel: 020-7942 5000

Science Museum ❻

Retrace your steps up Cromwell Road and turn left onto Exhibition Road. The Science Museum will be on your left. Founded in 1858 as part of the Victoria and Albert Museum, it became an independent entity in 1909. Its handsome symmetrical stone façade, with a Corinthian pediment, was designed by Sir Richard Allison. Displays include every kind of machine, from steam engines to spacecraft, exhibitions on weather, agriculture, shipping, mathematics, computing, and medicine, while the Wellcome Wing contains four floors of interactive technology and an IMAX cinema.

Science Museum
Opening times: 10am–6pm daily
Admission free
www.sciencemuseum.org.uk
Tel: 0333-241 4000

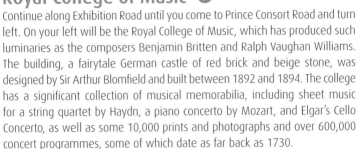

Royal College of Music

Continue along Exhibition Road until you come to Prince Consort Road and turn left. On your left will be the Royal College of Music, which has produced such luminaries as the composers Benjamin Britten and Ralph Vaughan Williams. The building, a fairytale German castle of red brick and beige stone, was designed by Sir Arthur Blomfield and built between 1892 and 1894. The college has a significant collection of musical memorabilia, including sheet music for a string quartet by Haydn, a piano concerto by Mozart, and Elgar's Cello Concerto, as well as some 10,000 prints and photographs and over 600,000 concert programmes, some of which date as far back as 1730.

The Royal College of Music's **Museum of Instruments** showcases more than 800 instruments and accessories dating from 1480 to the present, including the world's oldest keyboard instrument.

Museum of Instruments
Opening times: 8am–10pm daily
Admission free
www.rcm.ac.uk/museum
Tel: 020-7591 4300

Royal Albert Hall

Facing the Royal College of Music from the top of an imposing flight of steps is the rear of the Royal Albert Hall. This is one of England's most popular concert venues and home to the world-famous Proms Concerts every summer. It hosts more than 350 performances a year, everything from classical music and opera to rock and pop concerts, awards ceremonies, banquets, and even tennis tournaments. It is named in honour of Queen Victoria's husband, who planned to build a series of permanent educational facilities in this area, but died before any of them could be realised.

The red-brick exterior features an attractive terracotta frieze depicting *The Triumph of Arts and Sciences*. The hall's acoustics have always been bad – it has a notorious echo – and no attempts were even made to improve it until 1969, when a series of fibreglass discs were hung from the dome (which have been nicknamed the 'mushrooms' or 'flying saucers'). The magnificent organ has 9,999 pipes. The Proms, short for Promenade Concerts, is a series of popular musical evenings held over an eight-week period every summer; the Last Night of the Proms has become something of a national institution, with Union Jacks waving to the strains of Elgar's *Land of Hope and Glory*.

Kensington

Facing the Royal Albert Hall across Kensington Gore is the **Albert Memorial**. Commissioned by Queen Victoria after the death Prince Albert from typhoid in 1861 (he was only 41), it was designed by Sir George Gilbert Scott in an exuberant Gothic style, with a black-and-gold spire, a multi-coloured canopy made of marble, mosaics, enamels and wrought iron, some 200 sculptures, and, as its centrepiece, a gilded statue of the man himself.

> **Did You Know?**
> The statue of Prince Albert was painted black in 1915 when England was at war with Germany, and only re-gilded in 1998.

Royal Albert Hall
www.royalalberthall.com
Tel: 020-7589 8212

Albert Memorial

Royal College of Art ❾

Located next door to the Royal Albert Hall on Kensington Gore is the Modernist slab of the Royal College of Art. Founded in 1837, its pupils have included David Hockney, Peter Blake and Eduardo Paolozzi. The building is by Sir Hugh Casson and dates from 1962. Mainly glass-fronted, it makes for a startling contrast with the Victorian architecture that surrounds it.

Royal College of Art
www.rca.ac.uk
Tel: 020-7590 4444

Kensington Palace ❿

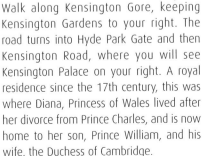

Walk along Kensington Gore, keeping Kensington Gardens to your right. The road turns into Hyde Park Gate and then Kensington Road, where you will see Kensington Palace on your right. A royal residence since the 17th century, this was where Diana, Princess of Wales lived after her divorce from Prince Charles, and is now home to her son, Prince William, and his wife, the Duchess of Cambridge.

Royal Albert Hall

Kensington

Originally built as Nottingham House for the Earl of Nottingham, it was bought from his heir to become King William III's London residence in 1689. The village of Kensington was considered to be far enough from the pollution of the city not to irritate the King's asthma. The palace was extended by Sir Christopher Wren with pavilions added at each corner of the central block. Royal Apartments were created, as well as the Great Stairs, a council chamber and the Chapel Royal. Wren also re-oriented the palace to face west, building north and south wings to flank the entryway, turning it into a court of honour.

The palace was the official residence of Britain's kings and queens for 70 years. In 1704 Sir John Vanbrugh designed an orangery for Queen Anne, while Henry Wise laid out a magnificent 12-hectare (30-acre) Baroque garden. George I then created lavish new Royal Apartments, including William Kent's Cupola Room in 1722. George II was the last king to live here, and it was he who had the gardens redesigned, removing the old-fashioned Baroque parterres. He also laid out the Serpentine lake, the Round Pond and the Broad Walk. From 1760 the Palace was used only by minor royalty, including the young Princess Victoria, who was living here when she became queen. Roughly half the palace is still home to royal apartments; the other half is open to the public.

Located on the Bayswater Road side of Kensington Gardens is the **Diana, Princess of Wales Memorial Playground**. Opened in 2000, this is the newest of Kensington Garden's three playgrounds, and takes its theme from the perennially popular Peter Pan. It has a cove, a 15-metre (50-foot) pirates' galleon, a tree house complete with walkways and ramps, and a mermaid's fountain with a half-submerged crocodile in it.

Kensington Palace
Opening times: 10am–6pm daily
Admission charges
www.hrp.org.uk/kensington-palace
Tel: 020-3166 6000

Diana, Princess of Wales Memorial Playground
Opening times: Daily 10am–3.45pm (Nov–Jan), to 4.45pm (Feb and late Oct), to 5.45pm (Mar and early Oct), to 6.45pm (Apr and Sep), to 7.45pm (May–Aug)
Admission free
www.royalparks.org.uk/parks/kensington-gardens/things-to-see-and-do/diana-memorial-playground

Notting Hill

Leave Kensington Gardens onto Bayswater Road and turn left. Kensington Palace Gardens will be on your left. This is a private road of large mansions occupying the former kitchen gardens of Kensington Palace. Halfway down, it turns into Palace Green, which has a number of embassies along it.

Continue along Bayswater Road as it turns into **Notting Hill Gate**. This is a cosmopolitan and fashionable part of London, its Victorian terraces home to an eclectic mix of wealthy, urbane Londoners (the 'mockneys', who love to flaunt their shabby-chic credentials) and Caribbean immigrants who moved here beginning in the 1950s. The area's original landowners were the Ladbroke family, who started developing the land in the 1820s. One of their great innovations was the layout of the communal gardens, which were accessible from the rear of the houses, instead of the more usual residential square separated from them by a road.

Kensington Palace

The **Notting Hill Carnival** is Europe's largest street festival and dates from the 1960s, when the area became home to immigrants from the Caribbean. It takes place over the August bank-holiday weekend.

Continue along Notting Hill Gate and turn right onto Pembridge Road; **Portobello Road** will be the second on your left. This is one of London's most famous street markets, specialising in antiques, jewellery, collectibles, and vintage clothing. The name Portobello comes from Puerto Bello in modern-day Panama, the scene of a popular British military victory over the Spanish in the mid-18th century. The market takes place on Saturdays and gets crowded during the summer.

Portobello Road
Antiques market: 8am–6.30pm Mon–Sat; admission free
www.portobelloroad.co.uk
Tel: 020-7361 3001

Holland Park ⑫

Retrace your steps to Notting Hill Gate and turn right. Continue until you come to the narrow laneway called Holland Walk, which will be on your left after Aubrey Road.

This leads to Holland Park. Holland Park covers approximately 22 hectares (55 acres) and is one of the quietest parks in the city. The northern half is covered in an almost untouched woodland; the central section is more formal, having once been the gardens of a great country house; the southern edge is used mainly for sporting activities; while the area around the park is one of the most fashionable residential areas, especially popular with celebrities who find it convenient for getting to the BBC in nearby Shepherd's Bush. It was a rural district until the 19th century, when the park came to be centred on a vast Jacobean house – **Holland House** – which, in the hands of the Third Baron Holland, served as a glittering centre for London's social life. Bombing destroyed most of the buildings during World War II; what remains now houses a restaurant, a youth hostel, a children's playground, tennis courts, a cricket pitch, an open-air theatre and a Japanese garden.

Follow Holland Walk and you will come to the **Design Museum** on your right on Kensington High Street. This museum was founded in 1989 and was first located in Shad Thames in London's Docklands, when it was the first museum in the world devoted solely to modern and contemporary design. Its new home is the former Commonwealth Institute building, a square-shaped 1960s building with a remarkable hyperbolic paraboloid roof clad in copper. Its interior galleries are arranged around a minimalist oak- and marble-lined atrium. Exhibitions explore landmarks in modern design history and change regularly. The museum embraces every area of design, from graphic design, fashion, furniture and architecture to cars.

Turn right onto Kensington High Street, then right again onto Melbury Road and left onto Holland Park Road and the **Leighton House Museum** will be on your right. This was the home of the 19th-century painter and sculptor Frederic Leighton. Designed by George Aitchison in a Neoclassical style in 1864, the house consisted of red brick and stone, and was extended and altered many times over the next 30 years. In 1877–79, the two-storey Arab Hall was added, to house Leighton's beautiful collection of Oriental tiles; the 16th- and 17th-century tiles are complemented by timber-latticework windows brought from Damascus and dating from the 17th century. The museum now houses works by Leighton as well as a number of other Pre-Raphaelite painters such as Millais, Burne-Jones and Watts.

Retrace your steps to Kensington High Street and turn left. Then take a left onto Phillimore Gardens and second right onto Stafford Terrace. **Linley Samborne House** will be on your right, at No. 18. This was the home of the *Punch* cartoonist Edward Linley Samborne. The house opened as a museum in 1980 and preserves the original furniture, art and décor.

Holland Park
Opening times: 7.30am–dusk daily
www.rbkc.gov.uk/leisure-and-culture/parks/holland-park

Design Museum
Opening times: 10am–6pm daily; admission free
www.designmuseum.org
Tel: 020-3862 5937

Leighton House Museum
Opening times: 10am–5.30pm daily; admission charges
www.rbkc.gov.uk/subsites/museums/leightonhousemuseum
Tel: 020-7602 3316

Linley Samborne House
Opening times: 2–5.30pm Wed, Sat and Sun (there are also guided tours by costumed guides – see website for details); admission charges
www.rbkc.gov.uk/subsites/museums/18staffordterrace
Tel: 020-7471 9158

Kensington Square ⓭

Continue along Stafford Terrace and turn right at the end onto Argyll Road. Turn left onto Kensington High Street, and **Kensington Roof Gardens** will be on your right. Accessible from No. 99 Kensington High Street, these were originally known as Derry and Toms Roof Gardens, and were laid out between 1936 and 1938 by landscape architect Ralph Hancock for the Barkers Department Store. They cover 6000 square metres (65,000 square feet), which makes them the largest roof gardens in Europe. A two-storey clubhouse sits at the centre and plays hosts to a variety of events. The gardens, which enjoy wonderful views over west London, are divided into three themed spaces: Spanish, based on the Alhambra; Tudor, with arches and fragrant flowering plants; and an English woodland garden, with trees, a stream, and a pond replete with ducks and flamingos.

Just behind Kensington Roof Gardens, down Derry Street, is **Kensington Square**, one of London's oldest. Laid out in the 1680s, it still has a few early 18th-century houses, including Nos. 11 and 12. The philosopher John Stuart Mill lived at No. 18, while the painter Edward Burne-Jones lived at No. 41.

Kensington Roof Gardens
Closed for renovations until 2020

Link to Chelsea walk: It is best get to Chelsea by tube. Return to Kensington High Street and turn left. The High Street Kensington tube station will be on your left just past Kensington Roof Gardens.

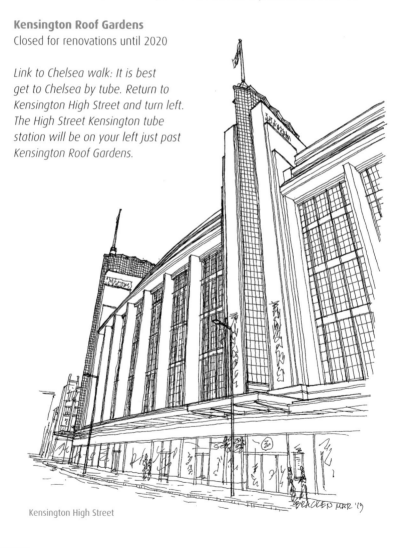

Kensington High Street

Chelsea

Nearest Tube: Sloane Square
Approximate walking time: 1 hour

Chelsea

Chelsea was an old Saxon village that became fashionable with Londoners escaping the city from the 16th century onwards. Its riverside atmosphere made it a welcome change from the oppressive noise and dirt of the metropolis, but it was still easily accessible by water. The Chelsea Physic Garden was founded here in 1673 by the Worshipful Company of Apothecaries while Christopher Wren's Royal Hospital was built between 1682 and 1689 as a home for retired soldiers; these veterans can still be seen sporting their scarlet coats and tricorn hats. In the 19th century the area became popular with intellectuals, including the poet Leigh Hunt, the historian Thomas Carlyle, the playwright Oscar Wilde and the writers Elizabeth Gaskell, George Eliot and Henry James, as well as the painters Dante Gabriel Rossetti and James Whistler. King's Road takes its name from a private road that used to link Hampton Court to London and it was where beautiful people could be seen strolling in front of trendy boutiques. The area is still fashionable, and, unusually for such a central part of town, retains its village-like feel.

CHELSEA

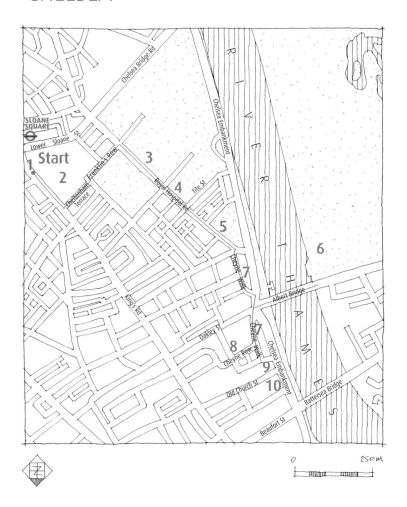

SLOANE SQUARE

Chelsea Bridge Rd

Lower Sloane St

Start

Franklin's Row

Cheltenham Terrace

Royal Hospital Rd

Tite St

Chelsea Embankment

RIVER

THAMES

King's Rd

Cheyne Walk

Albert Bridge

Oakley St

Cheyne Row

Cheyne Walk

Chelsea Embankment

Old Church St

Beaufort St

Battersea Bridge

1
2
3
4
5
6
7
8
9
10

0   250m

KEY

1. King's Road
2. Saatchi Gallery
3. Royal Hospital
4. National Army Museum
5. Chelsea Physic Garden
6. Battersea Park
7. Cheyne Walk
8. Carlyle's House
9. Chelsea Old Church
10. Roper's Garden

chelsea

King's Road ❶

Leave Sloane Square station and you will be on King's Road. Along with Carnaby Street, King's Road was one of the most fashionable parts of London in the 1960s and '70s: it was where the mini-skirt made its first appearance, and where the Punk movement was born. Still a popular shopping street, it is lined with a range of boutiques and good places to eat and drink, and is also an excellent place for browsing for antiques – although the prices are not particularly cheap. The Town Hall hosts temporary exhibitions and the occasional antiques fair; the Pheasantry, at No. 152, was built as a furniture-maker's shop in 1881 and is now a restaurant.

Sloane Square itself is a small, paved square, laid out in the late 18th century and named in honour of Sir Hans Sloane, doctor to George II, who bought Chelsea Manor in 1712. At the centre of Sloane Square you will find the Venus Fountain, whose basin depicts Charles II and his most colourful mistress, Nell Gwynn. The square is also home to the Peter Jones department store, a

Houses off King's Road (near Sloane Square)

stylish Modernist building dating from 1936 and an exemplar of what can be achieved with Modernist principles if only the architect will set his mind to it. The Royal Court Theatre, which sits opposite, is notable for fostering new drama.

Royal Court Theatre
www.royalcourttheatre.com
Tel: 020-7565 5000

Saatchi Gallery ❷

Walk along King's Road and turn left onto Cheltenham Terrace. On your left will be the Saatchi Gallery, one of London's most important galleries for contemporary art. This elegant Neoclassical former barracks is constructed in beige brick with a symmetrically placed Tuscan portico in Portland stone. Founded by the advertising magnate Charles Saatchi in 1985 to exhibit his private collection, the gallery features works by both famous names and newcomers, many of whom go on to become famous themselves. Damien Hirst, Tracy Emin and Jenny Saville have all been shown here.

Saatchi Gallery
Opening times: 10am–6pm daily; admission free
www.saatchigallery.com

Saatchi Gallery

chelsea

Royal Hospital

Royal Hospital ③

Continue along Cheltenham Terrace, which turns into Franklin's Row, and you will see the Royal Hospital ahead of you. Based on Louis XIV's Hôtel des Invalides in Paris, this military hospital and retirement home was commissioned by Charles II in 1681; the design, by Wren, for an elegantly symmetrical complex is also based on its Parisian predecessor. The first Chelsea pensioners were admitted in 1692, and the hospital is still home to about 330 retired soldiers today, all of whom wear the signature scarlet coats and tricorn hats that date from the 17th century. To be admitted a man must be a veteran, at least 65 years of age and single (many of them are widowers). Rooms are spartan, mainly because they haven't changed much in 300 years. The complex contains a small museum that outlines the hospital's history, as well as a statue of Charles II by Grinling Gibbons on the terrace. Since 1913, the Royal Hospital grounds have been the location of the world-famous Chelsea Flower Show.

Royal Hospital
Opening times: 10am–4pm Mon–Fri; admission free
www.chelsea-pensioners.co.uk
Tel: 020-7881 5257

National Army Museum

Located next door to the Royal Hospital is the National Army Museum, which highlights the history of the British Army from 1485 to the present, through paintings, tableaux, dioramas, archive film and interactive displays. Established in 1960, it got its Royal Charter that same year. Exhibits were originally displayed in the old riding school of the Royal Military Academy at Sandhurst before the museum moved in 1971 to this custom-built premises. The Modernist-Brutalist concrete building is designed by William Holford and Partners. There are cannon and other military hardware outside along the street, as well as a shop selling a range of military-themed books and the perennially popular toy soldier.

National Army Museum
Opening times: 10am–5.30pm daily; admission free
www.nam.ac.uk
Tel: 020-7730 0717

Chelsea Physic Garden

Continue along Royal Hospital Road and you will come to the Chelsea Physic Garden on your left, at No. 66. This was established by the Society of Apothecaries for the cultivation of plants for use in medicine in 1673, making it the second oldest botanical garden in England (after Oxford University's, established in 1621). The 18th century was a golden age for botanical studies, with the Chelsea Physic Garden becoming the world's best-stocked botanical garden. It also established a seed-exchange program with Leiden's famous botanical garden at the same time; this is still in operation. One of the garden's most famous propagations was the introduction of cotton to the American colony of Georgia. The garden was only opened to the public in 1983.

Chelsea Physic Garden
Opening times: 11am–6pm Sun–Fri (may vary in winter); admission charges
www.chelseaphysicgarden.co.uk
Tel: 020-7352 5646

Battersea Park

Continue along Royal Hospital Road and you will come to Chelsea Embankment. The **Albert Bridge** will be ahead of you. This was built in 1873 and is considered by many to be the prettiest of London's bridges – in fact it looks as if it is permanently ready for Christmas with all its fairy lights and tinselly décor. The sculpture at the traffic junction in front of it is called *Boy and Dolphin*, created by David Wynne in 1975.

Across the river lies **Battersea Park**, a duelling spot until the early 19th century. It was also a notorious area for vice, particularly around the Old

Red House pub. In an effort to clean up the area, and give Londoners a new green space for recreation, Sir James Pennethorne designed this park and linked it to central London via the Chelsea Bridge, which opened in 1858. The new park was immediately popular. Full of romantic gardens, a man-made boating lake and waterfalls, it later became a popular place for the late 19th-century craze for cycling. The park is also home to a small zoo, an art gallery, and the 35-metre (100-foot) Peace Pagoda overlooking the river.

Battersea Park
Opening times: 8am–dusk daily
Admission free
www.batterseapark.org
Tel: 020-8871 7530

Cheyne Walk ❼
Running parallel to Chelsea Embankment is Cheyne Walk. Once a pleasant riverside walkway, it was left inland when the Chelsea Embankment was

George Eliot's house, Cheyne Walk

built in 1874. Many of the houses in the area date from the early 18th century, and some of them are quite fine. The numerous blue plaques on the buildings bear testament to the area's popularity with London's intellectual elite in the 19th century: J.M.W. Turner lived incognito at No. 119, George Eliot died at No. 4, the writers Henry James, T.S. Eliot and Ian Fleming all lived in Carlyle Mansions, while on nearby Tite Street lived the Irish wit and playwright Oscar Wilde.

Carlyle's House ⑧

Located just off Cheyne Walk, at No. 24 Cheyne Row, is Carlyle's House. This is where the historian and philosopher Thomas Carlyle lived from 1834 until his death in 1882, and where he wrote many of his best-known books, including *The French Revolution* and *Frederick the Great*. The presence of such a literary luminary made the area fashionable and attracted London's leading literary and intellectual figures, including Dickens, Thackeray, Tennyson and Darwin. The house has been restored to look and feel just as it did in Carlyle's day.

Carlyle's House
Opening times: 11am–5pm Wed–Sun (Apr–Oct); admission free
www.nationaltrust.org.uk/carlyles-house

Chelsea Old Church ⑨

At the end of Cheyne Walk is Chelsea Old Church. This charming red-brick building was all but destroyed in World War II and has since been rebuilt. Also known as All Saints, this is a Church of England place of worship and dates from 1157. It was formerly the parish church of Chelsea village. The chancel was built in the 13th century, with the north and south chapels being added around 1325 and a tower as late as 1670. The chapels were originally private property. The northern one being known as the Lawrence Chapel, owned by Chelsea's Lord of the Manor, and the southern one being rebuilt in 1528 as Sir Thomas More's private chapel. There is a statue of More designed by Leslie Cubitt Bevis in 1969 outside the church facing the river.

Chelsea Old Church
Opening times: 2–4pm Tue–Thur; admission free
www.chelseaoldchurch.org.uk
Tel: 020-7795 1019

Roper's Garden ⑩

Located just behind Chelsea Old Church is Roper's Garden, named after Sir Thomas More's daughter Margaret Roper (her husband William wrote More's

Chelsea Old Church

biography). The garden is believed to have existed for centuries. Small but charming and beautifully planted, it contains a lovely old cherry tree commemorating the visit of Gunji Koizumi, the man who introduced judo to England around 1900. There is also a sculpture by Jacob Epstein, who had his studio here between 1909 and 1914.

The **Old Dairy**, nearby at No. 46 Old Church Street, was built in 1796 at a time when cows still grazed the surrounding fields. The dairy's tiling is original.

End of walks

Further Afield

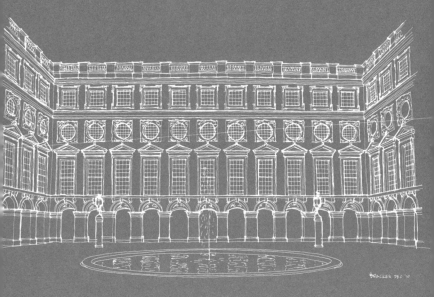

Further Afield

This chapter covers districts and specific buildings and places that are a little out of the city centre, or that do not fall conveniently into any of the city walks. This includes three Georgian-era villages – Hampstead, Greenwich and Richmond – as well as some of their adjoining areas and attractions, such as Highgate, the O2 complex, the London Docklands, Kew Gardens and Hampton Court. It also includes the Dulwich Picture Gallery, to the south, and several museums dotted around the East End, such as the Geffrye Museum, the V&A Museum of Childhood, the William Morris Gallery and Sutton House.

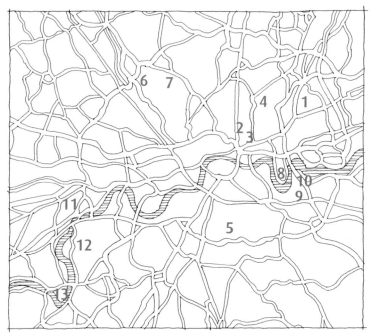

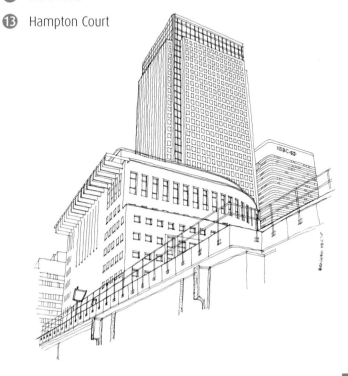

Further Afield

Geffrye Museum ❶
Tube: Hoxton

Leave Hoxton station via Cremer Street and turn right onto Kingsland Road. The Geffrye Museum will be on your right. This lovely museum, housed in a set of converted almshouses, is dedicated to showing the changing face of the English domestic interior. It begins with the Elizabethan period (which contains some wonderful panelling) and runs through various decorative styles down to the present day. Each room contains excellent examples of its period's furniture, with a focus on the homes of ordinary people – making for a refreshing change from the splendours of aristocratic living more usually seen in museums. A popular annual exhibition is 'Christmas Past', where each room is decorated for the festive season.

Geffrye Museum
Closed for renovations until Spring 2020
www.geffrye-museum.org.uk
Tel: 020-7739 9893

V&A Museum of Childhood ❷
Tube: Bethnal Green

Leave Bethnal Green station and walk up Cambridge Heath Road, keeping Victoria Park Gardens on your right. The Victoria and Albert Museum of Childhood has the largest collection of childhood-related objects in the country. The toys, games and costumes, as well as dolls' houses, model trains and theatres, date from the 16th century to the present day. The upper floor has activities which children should find fun, such as a dressing-up area and a fairground mirror.

Sutton House, Homerton

V&A Museum of Childhood
Opening times: 10am–5.45pm daily; admission free
www.vam.ac.uk/moc
Tel: 020-8983 5200

Sutton House ❸
Tube: Homerton
Leave Homerton station via Sedgwick Street and turn right onto Homerton High Street. On your left, at Nos. 2–4, will be Sutton House, the oldest residential building in this part of the city. Built in 1535, and though modified during the Georgian era, the house remains essentially Tudor, with some Tudor windows, oak linen-fold panelling, and large carved fireplaces. The house's interesting exhibits recount its long history, as home to merchants, sea captains, silk-weavers, schoolmistresses, and clergy. Sutton House was bought by the National Trust in the 1930s thanks to a bequest, and it managed to survive the war only to fall into disrepair and be squatted during the 1980s.

Sutton House
Opening times: noon–4.30pm daily; admission free
www.nationaltrust.org.uk/sutton-house-and-breakers-yard
Tel: 020-8986 2264

William Morris Gallery ❹
Tube: Walthamstow Central
Leave Walthamstow Central station and turn right up Hoe Street. Turn left onto Jewel Road and the William Morris Gallery will be at the end, overlooking Forest Road. Morris was an artist, designer, writer, craftsman and socialist, one of the

William Morris Gallery

leading lights of the Arts and Crafts movement. Born in 1834, he lived with his parents in this charming country house between 1848 and 1856. It opened as a museum in 1950. The gallery illustrates his considerable influence on the English arts scene, with displays of fabrics, carpets, wallpapers, furniture, stained glass and tiles designed by him and his contemporaries. It also exhibits several works of Geoffrey Chaucer printed by Morris's Kelmscott Press.

William Morris Gallery
Opening times: 10am–5pm Tue–Sun; admission free
www.wmgallery.org.uk
Tel: 020-8496 4390

Dulwich Picture Gallery ❺

Rail: West Dulwich
Leave the West Dulwich railway station and turn right onto Thurlow Park Road. Then turn left onto Gallery Road and the Dulwich Picture Gallery will be on your right after the tennis club. Opened in 1817, this was the first purpose-built public art gallery in England. The collection was assembled by Sir Francis Bourgeois and Noel Desenfans, who ran an art dealership in London and had been asked to put together a royal collection for the king of Poland in 1790. Five years later they had done so, but Poland no longer existed – it had been swallowed up by neighbours Russia and Prussia. The collection was eventually willed to Dulwich College, with the stipulation by Bourgeois that a museum to display the paintings was to be established and had to be designed by his friend John Soane. The gallery's impressive collection includes works by Rembrandt (notably his *Jacob II de Gheyn*, which has been stolen four times), Canaletto, Poussin, Watteau, Murillo and Raphael.

Dulwich Picture Gallery
Opening times: 10am–5pm Tue–Sun; admission charges
www.dulwichpicturegallery.org.uk
Tel: 020-8693 5254

Hampstead ❻

Tube: Hampstead
Hampstead is a pretty Georgian village nestling amid the hills north of the city, adjacent to a magnificent heath. A combination of its proximity to London and its distinctly village-like feel has made Hampstead a popular place with the rich and artistic over the centuries; it has been home to people like John Constable, John Keats, D.H. Lawrence, J.B. Priestly and Kingsley Amis.

Keats House

Leave Hampstead tube station and follow Rosslyn Hill until you come to **Downshire Hill** and turn left. This charming street of Regency houses has

long been a popular gathering place for artists, with the Pre-Raphaelites Dante Gabriel Rossetti and Edward Burne-Jones meeting at No. 47 – which is also where Stanley Spencer and Mark Gertler used to meet during the 1920s and '30s.

Turn right onto Keats Grove. The church on the corner was built in 1823 and still contains its original pews. **Keats House** will be on the right-hand side. Built in 1814–16, this was one of the first houses to be built in the area – originally as two semi-detached homes. Keats moved into the smaller one in 1818, and lived there for two years, during which he is said to have written his lovely 'Ode to a Nightingale' while sitting under a plum tree in the garden. He became engaged to Fanny Brawne during this time. She lived next door. Keats moved to Italy in an effort to stave off his tuberculosis but died there in 1820, at the age of only 25. He and Fanny never married. On display at this touching little museum are one of Keats's love letters, his engagement ring to Fanny, and a lock of her hair.

Keats House
Opening times: 11am–5pm Wed–Sun; admission charges
www.cityoflondon.gov.uk/things-to-do/keats-house

Well Walk & Flask Walk

Return to Downshire Hill and turn right, then take a left on East Heath Road; **Well Walk** will be on your left. There was a therapeutic spa located here in the 18th century, whose water, rich in iron salts, was sold in flasks here and in London. A disused fountain now marks the site of the old well. The Wells Tavern used to be a popular trysting place but Well Walk also had its more respectable side, where John Constable, D.H. Lawrence, J.B. Priestly and John Keats all once made their homes.

Well Walk turns into **Flask Walk**, which is named after the Flask Pub. Flask Walk narrows as it approaches High Street and is lined with interesting little shops. Once past the Victorian pub it broadens out into a handsome Regency street and this was where the novelist Kingsley Amis used to live.

At the point where Well Walk turns into Flask Walk sits **Burgh House**, home to the Hampstead Museum. (The entrance is on New End Square.) Built in 1702–03, this fine Queen Anne house boasts a magnificent carved wooden staircase from the period, but is otherwise much altered. The music room is a reconstruction from 1920 but contains some excellent 18th-century panelling (which came from another house). There is a room devoted to John Constable, and exhibitions on Lawrence, Keats and the artist Stanley Spencer.

Burgh House
Opening times: Noon–5pm Wed–Fri and Sun; admission free
www.burghhouse.museumssites.com
Tel: 020-7431 0144

Fenton House, Hampstead

Church Row

Continue along Flask Walk until you come back out onto Rosslyn Hill and turn right. Then take the sharp left onto Heath Street and the **Everyman Cinema** will be on your right, at No. 5 Holly Bush Vale. This building first opened in the 1880s as the Hampstead Drill Hall and Assembly Rooms. Later it was converted into a theatre, the Everyman Theatre, which operated from 1920 until 1933, when it became a cinema. It is still popular with the art-house crowd today.

Continue along Heath Street and **Church Row** will be on your right. This is one of the finest and most intact Georgian streets in the whole of London. The western end is home to St John's church, with its gorgeous iron railings, which holds a bust of John Keats, and the grave of John Constable in the churchyard.

Turn right off Church Row onto Holly Walk and then right again onto Mount Vernon. Follow this street as it veers to the left and you will come to Windmill Hill. The garden entrance to **Fenton House** will be in front of you (the main entrance is around the corner at No. 20 Hampstead Grove). This wonderful William and Mary house was built in 1686 and is the oldest house in Hampstead. It is open during the summer and houses two fascinating exhibitions: the Benton-Fletcher collection of early keyboard instruments – which includes a harpsichord dating from 1612 said to have been played by Handel – and a fine collection of porcelain, amassed by Lady Binning, who bequeathed the house and its contents to the National Trust in 1952. The house itself – with its mellow red brick and lightly expressed Neoclassical detailing – as well as the wonderful garden, make this a real treat to visit.

Everyman Cinema
www.everymancinema.com
Tel: 0871-906 9060

Fenton House
Opening times: 11am–5pm Wed–Sun (Apr–Oct); admission free
www.nationaltrust.org.uk/fenton-house-and-garden
Tel: 020-7435 3471

Hampstead Heath

Follow Hampstead Grove and turn right onto Admiral's Walk. **Admiral's House**, built for a sea captain around 1700, takes its name from the maritime motifs on its exterior, although no admiral is known to have ever lived here. Next door is **Grove Lodge**, home of the novelist John Galsworthy for the last 15 years of his life.

Continue along Admiral's Walk and you will come back out onto Heath Street. Turn left and you will arrive at **Hampstead Heath**. This is a popular place to stroll in the day, but can be a bit unsavoury at night – so beware. It commands wonderful views and links Hampstead to neighbouring Highgate across the hill. With everything from woods and meadows to hills, ponds and lakes, it is one of London's most spectacular and varied open spaces, and can get crowded on days with good weather. The **Vale of Heath** was originally a swamp until it was drained in 1770 and became something of a health resort popular with people who could afford to flee London and its various outbreaks of disease such as cholera and typhoid. The poet James Henry Leigh Hunt established a salon here in 1815, with guests like Coleridge, Byron, Shelley and Keats, making the area even more fashionable. The **Old Bull and Bush**, on North End Road, is one of London's most famous pubs – a literary and artistic haunt, attracting the likes of William Hogarth. The charming **Hill Garden** was laid out by Lord Leverhulme, the wealthy soap magnate; it now forms part of Hampstead Heath and contains a pretty pergola and formal pond.

Old Bull and Bush
Tel: 020-8905 5456

The Hill Garden
Opening times: 8.50am–dusk daily; admission free
Tel: 020-7332 3322

Highgate ❼
Tube: Highgate
There has been a settlement at Highgate since the early Middle Ages. It takes its name from the gated staging post that was established on the Great North

Road. Like Hampstead, it became fashionable in the 18th century for those seeking to escape the squalor of London. With its hilly aspect, clean air and village-like feel, it was a sought-after residential area. It still is today, though not quite as exclusive as its neighbour across the Heath. Highgate was where Dick Whittington, the disheartened young country lad who was about to leave London, was persuaded to stay by the tolling of the Bow Bells in the distance; he and his cat went back into the city, where he made his fortune and went on to became Lord Mayor. There is a statue of a black cat on Highgate Hill to mark this epiphany.

Highgate Cemetery
Tube: Archway
From Archway station walk up the very steep Highgate Hill and turn left onto Bradfield Road which turns into Magdala Avenue. Turn left at the end onto Dartmouth Park Hill and right onto Raydon Street. You will see the eastern part of Highgate Cemetery on your right where Raydon Street turns into Chester Road. This is London's most famous cemetery and is the resting place for the likes of Karl Marx, George Eliot, and Douglas Adams. The tombstones in the western portion reflect the mawkishness of the high-Victorian era. There are lots of broken columns (symbolising a life cut short), despondent-looking angels and flowery inscriptions. It is an extremely evocative and atmospheric place, hilly, overgrown in places and full of lovely trees. It lay neglected for years until the Friends of Highgate Cemetery was established, who set out to save it from further decline.

Highgate Cemetery
East Cemetery: Free admission
West Cemetery: By guided tour only, 10.30am–3pm Sat and Sun;
admission charges
www.highgatecemetery.org
Tel: 020-8340 1834

Highgate Cemetery

Freud Museum

Tube: Finchley Road

Leave Finchley Road tube station and cross Finchley Road onto Netherhall Gardens. Turn right onto Nutley Terrace and right again onto Maresfield Gardens; the Freud Museum will be on your left, at No. 20. This is where the Viennese doctor and founder of psychoanalysis came to live when fleeing the Nazi annexation of Austria in 1938. The lovely Queen Anne-style house, built in 1920, remained in the Freud family until their youngest daughter Anna died in 1982. It opened as a museum in 1986 and its centrepiece is Freud's study – complete with his iconic couch. The museum also organises research and publication programmes, seminars and conferences.

Freud Museum
Opening times: Noon–5pm Wed–Sun; admission charges
www.freud.org.uk
Tel: 020-7435 2002

The Jewish Museum

Tube: Camden Town

Leave Camden Town station and follow Parkway until you come to Albert Street and turn left. The Jewish Museum will be on your right, at Nos. 129–31. The exhibits celebrate Jewish life in the British Isles since the Middle Ages, with an important collection of ceremonial art, including Hanukkah lamps, wedding rings and illuminated marriage contracts. The museum's highlight has to be the 16th-century synagogue ark, which comes from Venice. A Holocaust Gallery shows filmed testimony from one of the few British people to be interned at Auschwitz.

The Jewish Museum
Opening times: 10am–5pm Sat–Thur, 10am–2pm Fri; admission charges
www.jewishmuseum.org.uk
Tel: 020-7284 7384

Docklands ⑧

Tube: Canary Wharf
DLR: West India Quay

Canary Wharf is London's newest business district and forms a counterbalance to the older City of London. An impressive cluster of skyscrapers rises from the ruins of the West India Docks – once part of the world's busiest port but closed down in 1980 after newer facilities were built downstream at Tilbury. One Canada Square, designed by Cesar Pelli, was the country's tallest building when it was built in 1991, at 50 storeys, or 230 metres (770 feet) tall.

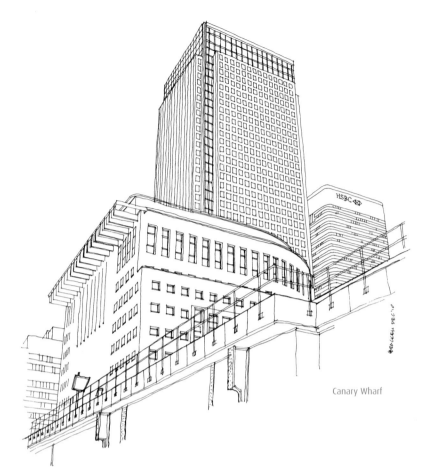

Canary Wharf

The **Museum of London Docklands** is located at the No. 1 Warehouse, West India Quay. This late-Georgian warehouse used to house sugar from the West Indies. The museum opened in 2003 and shows the history of the Port of London from Roman times to the present day. There is also a children's gallery and a study centre where the public can consult the museum's archives.

Information Centre, Museum of London Docklands
Opening times: 10am–6pm daily; admission free
www.museumoflondon.org.uk/museum-london-docklands
Tel: 020-7001 9844

Greenwich ❾
DLR: Cutty Sark
Greenwich is another of the pretty Georgian-era villages on the outskirts of London. A World Heritage site, it is perhaps most famous for having given its name to Greenwich Mean Time, because it is the place from which all of the world's time zones are measured. Traditionally the eastern approach to London by water, Greenwich is home to the National Maritime Museum and the Old

Royal Naval College, which are best seen from the river; while Greenwich Park is home to Inigo Jones's Renaissance masterpiece, the Queen's House. The village itself is full of lovely shops, many of them specialising in antiques and books, as well as cafés and restaurants. It is also home to the Wernher Collection and the Fan Museum.

It is possible to get to Greenwich from the Docklands via the **Greenwich Foot Tunnel**. This 370-metre (1,200-foot) tunnel was opened in 1902 to allow labourers to get from south London to work in the Millwall Docks. Round, red-brick terminals with glass domes mark the lift shafts at both ends of the tunnel. At the Greenwich end is the **Cutty Sark**, recently restored after a disastrous fire. This ship was launched as a tea clipper in 1869. Clippers were the speedy vessels that shipped products like tea from China for the increasingly insatiable markets of the United Kingdom in the 19th century. This particular ship won the annual clippers' race from China to London in 1871, making the journey in just 107 days. It only stopped sailing in 1938 and has been on display here since 1957.

Greenwich Foot Tunnel
Open 24 hours daily

Cutty Sark
Opening times: 10am–5pm daily; admission charges
www.rmg.co.uk/cutty-sark

Old Royal Naval College

This magnificent complex overlooking the River Thames is one of the stateliest Baroque ensembles in the whole of Europe. Begun by John Webb in 1664–69, it was continued by Sir Christopher Wren between 1696 and 1716, with the west front being completed by Sir John Vanbrugh. The complex features carved details by Nicholas Hawksmoor and paintings by James Thornhill. Wren's great genius was to create the Charles II block, making a magnificent vista that centres on the serene Renaissance beauty of Inigo Jones's Queen's House. The college's dramatic colonnades were inspired by Perrault's east front of the Louvre in Paris. The original chapel, by Wren, was gutted in a fire in 1779; James Stuart's replacement is in a lighter Greek Revival style. The statue at the centre of the complex's courtyard is of George II – depicted as a Roman emperor. A visually stunning complex to wander around.

Beside the Old Royal Naval College, and also overlooking the river, is **Trafalgar Tavern**. This was one of Charles Dickens's old haunts. He used to drink here with his illustrator George Cruikshank. Opened in 1837, the pub was a popular venue for London's famous 'whitebait dinners'. These were when London notables would come to feast on this tiny but delicious fish. Though no longer fished in the Thames, whitebait can still be found on the menu here.

Old Royal Naval College
Opening times: 10am–5pm daily; admission free
www.ornc.org
Tel: 020-8269 2131

Trafalgar Tavern
www.trafalgartavern.co.uk
Tel: 020-3887 9886

Queen's House

From the Old Royal Naval College complex exit onto Romney Road. The Queen's House sits on axis with the College at the edge of Greenwich Park. Built in two phases – the first, between 1614 and 1617, for Anne of Denmark, wife of James I, and the second, almost twenty years later, for Henrietta Maria, wife of Charles I – the house contains galleries displaying the National Maritime Museum's art collection.

This building is without a doubt one of the most important in the history of British architecture. It was one of Inigo Jones's first commissions after returning to England from his Grand Tour of Italy. With it he introduced the Palladian style to the country. Hitherto the English had simply applied Neoclassical details to their buildings, not really understanding their significance; Jones's work was the first where an entire house was planned according to Neoclassical principles – with a strict system of proportions and the correct use of the classical orders – and it proved hugely influential, not just in England, but all over the world, thanks to the British Empire. The house's importance to subsequent architects can be seen from the way it sits as the central focus of the Old Royal Naval College complex, which frames it dramatically when seen from the river – a suitable homage to this most influential of buildings by the masters who followed him.

Located next door to the Queen's House is the **National Maritime Museum**. Built in the 19th century as a school for sailors' children, it opened as a museum in 1937. Highlighting the vital role the sea has played in Britain's history, exhibits tell the story of Elizabethan explorers, 18th- and 19th-century empire-builders and 20th- and 21st-century shipping. The expeditions of Cook and Shackleton are outlined, as are the campaigns of Lord Nelson. The exhibition even includes the bloodstained clothes Nelson was wearing when he was fatally shot at the Battle of Trafalgar in 1805.

Queen's House
Opening times: 10am–5pm daily; admission free
www.rmg.co.uk/queens-house

National Maritime Museum
Opening times: 10am–5pm daily; admission free
www.rmg.co.uk/national-maritime-museum

Greenwich Park

This was originally the grounds of a royal palace and is still a royal park. André Le Nôtre, who worked on Versailles, designed a layout for it in the 17th century – the broad avenue was part of this plan. The hilltop commands stunning views of the city and the river, especially the Queen's House centred on the Old Royal Naval College and the towers of Canary Wharf in the distance.

The top of the hill is also home to the **Royal Observatory**. This was established as the government observatory in 1675 – when it was suitably distant from the bright lights of London to allow for astronomical observations – and remained such until 1948, when the observatory moved to Sussex. The house now contains a display of John Harrison's famous marine timekeepers, an exhibition on Greenwich Mean Time, and a planetarium.

The southern part of Greenwich Park turns into **Blackheath**, a pretty area of up-market Georgian terraces and home to a number of shops selling books and antiques. Long the place where angry mobs would gather before entering London to protest, this is where Wat Tyler's band of rebels gathered before the Peasants' Revolt of 1381.

Greenwich Park
Opening times: 6am–dusk daily
www.royalparks.org.uk/parks/greenwich-park
Tel: 0300-061 2380

Royal Observatory
Opening times: 10am–5pm daily; admission free
www.rmg.co.uk/royal-observatory

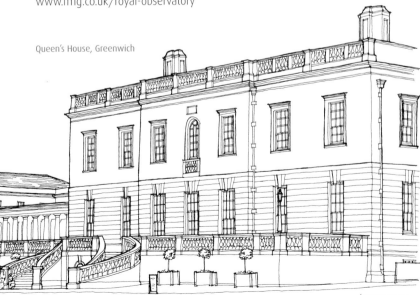

Queen's House, Greenwich

Ranger's House
(Wernher Collection)

This charming mansion is located on Chesterfield Walk, at the western edge of Greenwich Park. Built in 1688, this elegant, almost perfectly symmetrical red-brick building became home in 1815 to the Royal Parks' ranger. Today it showcases the Wernher Collection, an impressive collection of paintings, furniture, jewellery and porcelain as amassed by the South African diamond miner Sir Julius Wernher. Highlights include masterpieces by Hans Memling and Filippo Lippi, as well as Gothic ivories and Renaissance jewels and bronzes. The rose garden is a particular delight.

Exit Greenwich Park onto **Croom's Hill** and you will be on one of London's best-kept 17th-century streets. The oldest buildings are located at the southern end, near Blackheath, with an original Manor House dating from 1695 (at No. 68), and an even older house located at No. 66.

Follow Croom's Hill as it winds its way downhill and you will come to the **Fan Museum** at No. 12. This is one of London's more unusual museums – in fact it is the only one of its kind in the world. Opened in 1991, it is home to Helene Alexander's personal collection of 3,500 fans – the earliest of which dates from the 17th century.

Continue along Croom's Hill as it turns into Stockwell Street and you will see the **St Alfege Church** ahead of you. Completed in 1714 on the site of an older church, this is one of Nicholas Hawksmoor's masterpieces. Gigantic columns grace the façade, supporting massive pediments topped by urns – all quite exuberantly Baroque. Some of the interior wood carving is by Grinling Gibbons; a lot of it was damaged during World War II, but has since been restored.

Across Greenwich Church Street from St Alfege Church is the charming **Greenwich Market**, a good place for browsing or taking a break to have something to eat or drink.

Wernher Collection
Opening times: 11am–5pm Sun–Thur; admission charges
www.english-heritage.org.uk/visit/places/rangers-house-the-wernher-collection
Tel: 0370-333 1181

Fan Museum
Opening times: 11am–5pm Tue–Sat; noon–5pm Sun; admission charges
www.thefanmuseum.org.uk
Tel: 020-8305 1441

St Alfege Church
Opening times: 11am–4pm Mon–Sat, 11am–noon Sun; admission free
www.st-alfege.org
Tel: 020-8853 0687

Greenwich Market
Opening times: 10am–5.30pm daily
www.greenwichmarket.london
Tel: 020-8269 5096

The O2 ❿
Tube: North Greenwich
Originally known as the Millennium Dome, this was one of the focal points of Britain's millennium celebrations. Somehow though, it never quite caught the public's imagination the way the London Eye did. It is now used as a concert arena and includes bars, restaurants, a cinema, a sports arena and IndigO2, a smaller concert venue. This massive arena's roof is held in place by twelve 100-metre (328-foot) support towers, and is the world's largest single-roof structure, with a diameter of 365 metres (1,197 feet). The number of the towers and the measurement of the diameter are references to Greenwich's role as the international meridian.

The O2
www.theo2.co.uk
Tel: 020-8463 2000

Kew Gardens ⓫
Tube or rail: Kew Gardens
Leave Kew Gardens station and follow the signs for Kew Gardens along Lichfield Road. This is one of the world's most famous botanical gardens and a World Heritage site. Kew contains the world's largest collection of living plants, with more than 30,000 different varieties, and is dotted with a number of pretty buildings, including Neoclassical temples and a Chinese pagoda. The library holds more than 750,000 volumes, as well as some 175,000 prints and drawings of plants.

The gardens were planned by Sir William Chambers for Frederick, Prince of Wales, in 1751, but all of the buildings Chambers designed have since been demolished, with the exception of his Chinese pagoda – which looks, quite frankly, as authentically Chinese as a plate of fish and chips. George III further enriched the gardens, with the able assistance of the director Sir Joseph Banks; it was Banks who really did the most to establish Kew's international reputation. One of the garden's most famous sights is the Palm House. When it was built in 1844–1848, it was the first large-scale structure to make use of wrought iron, and the 16,000 panes of glass were originally hand-blown. This jewel of Victorian engineering, with its delicately curved structure, is home to Kew's collection of tropical plants. Its design, by Decimus Burton, influenced not only glasshouses around the world but also Joseph Paxton's Crystal Palace for the Great Exhibition of 1851.

Temple, Kew Gardens

The Temperate House dates from 1899 and is where delicate woodland plants are housed, according to their geographical origins. The Davies Alpine House is a high-tech structure by Wilkinson Eyre. The first Alpine House was built at Kew in 1887. Originally of timber and brick, its successor stood from 1981 to 2004. The present replacement is a sustainable and energy-efficient building that recreates Alpine habitats. Its twin-arched structure contains 211 glass panels and stands 11.5 metres (38 feet) tall.

Kew Gardens
Opening times: From 10am daily (closing times vary); admission charges
www.kew.org
Tel: 020-8332 5655

Syon House
Wander Kew Gardens at leisure and exit by turning left onto Kew Road. Follow it all the way to the river and cross it and you will see **Strand on the Green** on your right-hand side. This charming riverside walkway passes a number of fine 18th-century houses as well as more modest fishermen's cottages. The City Barge is the oldest of the three pubs, parts of it dating back to the 15th century. Its name comes from the fact that the Lord Mayor's barge used to moor here.

On the other side of Kew Road is Kew Bridge Road and on the right-hand side of it is the **London Museum of Water and Steam** (just after Green

Dragon Lane). This 19th-century water-pumping station is now a museum highlighting the uses to which steam power and water were put in London. The main exhibit is the five huge Cornish beam engines that used to pump water from the river here. This was then distributed throughout London. The earliest engines, some of which date from 1820, were similar to those that were used to pump water out of Cornwall's tin mines. They can be seen in operation during weekends and public holidays.

Continue along Kew Bridge Road and you will come to the **Musical Museum** on your right, at No. 399 High Street. This collection of large musical instruments ranges over three floors and includes automatic pianos and organs, as well as miniature and cinema pianos. It also contains what it believed to be the only surviving self-playing Wurlitzer organ in Europe.

Continue along High Street as it turns into London Road and you will come to **Syon House** on your left. The Dukes of Northumberland have lived in this stately home for more than four centuries, making it one of only a few important houses in London still in hereditary ownership. The exterior is somewhat plain – almost reminiscent of a child's toy fort in fact, with its barrack-like windows and unconvincing battlements – but the interior is magnificent. Remodelled by Robert Adam between 1762 and 1769, it is considered to be one of the masterpieces of 18th-century interior decoration. Working within the considerable limitations of Tudor planning, Adam showed considerable genius in overcoming the lack of space and the awkwardly shaped rooms. He divided the irregular shape of the Great Hall into three sections by creating apses at either end and allowing a correctly proportioned Neoclassical hall in the middle. In the anteroom he made use of a screen to turn what had been a rectangular room into a square one. His bold use of colour is also amply demonstrated. The 80-hectare (200-acre) park was remodelled at the same time by Lancelot 'Capability' Brown, with a 16-hectare (40-acre) garden containing more than 200 rare species of trees.

London Museum of Water and Steam
Opening times: 10am–4pm Wed–Sun; admission charges
www.waterandsteam.org.uk
Tel: 020-8568 4757

Musical Museum
Opening times: 10.30am–5pm Tue, Fri–Sun; admission charges
www.musicalmuseum.co.uk
Tel: 020-8560 8108

Syon House
Opening times: 11am–5pm daily (gardens open 10.30am); admission charges
www.syonpark.co.uk
Tel: 020-8560 0882

Osterley Park House
Tube: Osterley

Leave Osterley tube station and turn left onto Great West Road. Turn left again onto Thornbury and the entrance to the Osterley estate will be straight ahead of you. Originally an Elizabethan manor house built by Sir Thomas Gresham (founder of the Royal Exchange) in the 1570s, it fell into disrepair and was rebuilt in an elegantly symmetrical Neoclassical style by Robert Adam in the 1760s and is rightly regarded as one of his masterpieces. Its signature Ionic portico (which looks like a colonnade and is most unusual) as well as the ceiling in the library are evidence of an architect at the height of his powers, while the corner towers, with their ogee roofs, hark back to the original Elizabethan manor house. Much of the house's furniture was also designed by Adam, as was the garden house. The garden and its temple, however, were designed by William Chambers. The estate passed into the hands of the Earls of Jersey through marriage, and the Ninth Earl gave it to the National Trust after World War II.

Osterley Park House
Opening times: Noon–4pm daily (grounds 7am–7.30pm daily)
Admission charges
www.nationaltrust.org.uk/osterley
Tel: 020-8232 5050

Chiswick House
Rail: Chiswick

Leave Chiswick railway station by turning right onto Burlington Lane and you will come to Chiswick House on your left. Inspired by the villas of ancient Rome, this Neoclassical house has an almost doll's-house perfection, and was designed by its owner Richard Boyle, the Earl of Burlington, with the assistance of architect William Kent. Burlington so revered Palladio and his disciple Inigo Jones that statues of the two men adorn the outside of the villa. The house is organised around a central octagonal room – clearly based on Palladio's Villa Rotunda (but using Corinthian instead of Ionic columns). One of the most distinctive features of the house is its geometric planning, with rooms designed to be perfect squares, rectangles or circles in plan, and often perfect cubes or double cubes in volume. In deliberate contrast to the monochromatic exterior, the interiors are lavishly decorated. Burlington purchased building materials while in Italy and these lend the villa a further sense of authenticity.

Continue along Burlington Lane until you come to Paxton Road and turn left. At the end of this street, which veers sharply to the right, make a right turn onto Hogarth Lane and you will see **Hogarth's House** on the right. William Hogarth lived here from 1749 until his death in 1764 and called it 'a little country box by the Thames'. He often painted pretty country

scenes from its windows. The house suffered damage during World War II, followed by years of neglect, but has since been turned into a small museum and gallery featuring engraved copies of Hogarth's most famous works, including *The Rake's Progress* (the originals of which can be seen in Sir John Soane's Museum).

Chiswick House
Opening times: 11am–3pm Mon and Wed, 11am–4pm Sat and Sun (gardens 7am–dusk daily)
Admission charges (gardens are free)
www.chiswickhouseandgardens.org.uk
Tel: 0203-141 3351

Hogarth's House
Opening times: Noon–5pm Tue–Sun; admission free
Tel: 020-8994 6757

Pitzhanger Manor House and Gallery
Tube: Ealing Broadway
Leave Ealing Broadway station by turning left onto the Broadway, which veers to the right where it meets the Mall. Turn left onto High Street and right onto Mattock Lane. The Pitzhanger Manor House and Gallery will be on your left. This house was designed by Sir John Soane in 1803 as his country residence. It replaced an older house, and even though Soane retained the drawing room and dining room (which were designed by George Dance the Younger in 1768), the rest of the house clearly bears Soane's idiosyncratic stamp, particularly the library, the breakfast room and the 'monk's dining room'. The gallery displays contemporary art, as well as an exhibition of Martinware, a sort of highly decorative glazed pottery that was made in Southall between 1877 and 1915 and extremely fashionable in the late Victorian era. The manor's gardens are now a pleasant public park.

Pitzhanger Manor House and Gallery
Opening times: 10am–4.30pm Tue–Fri, 10am–3pm Sat, 10am–4.30pm Sun
Admission charges
www.pitzhanger.org.uk
Tel: 020-3994 0966

Richmond ⑫
Tube or rail: Richmond
Richmond's full name is Richmond upon Thames and it is one of the three pretty Georgian villages that lie on the outskirts of London (the other two being Hampstead and Greenwich). Located at a particularly pleasant meandering

part of the Thames, Richmond is a popular place to escape the city during the summer, especially for those who are fond of water sports. The area has long been popular with artists and writers, including George Eliot, and, more recently, pop stars, such as members of the Rolling Stones and The Who.

Marble Hill House

Follow Kew Road as it turns into Hill Street and then turn right onto Richmond Road as it crosses the river. Follow this road as it veers to the left, and on your left will be Marble Hill House, one of London's finest examples of Palladian architecture, built in 1729 for Henrietta Howard, the Countess of Pembroke. Architect Roger Morris's clean lines and elegant symmetry are strictly Palladian, but the interior reveals the more usual Anglo-Palladian hybrid, with much of the symmetry being the result of trickery (false doors, etc.). The countess was a well-known intellectual and held a salon in the Great Room, the most striking part of the interior; all the other rooms were made to seem small by comparison. The gardens were landscaped by Charles Bridgeman, with the assistance of the poet Alexander Pope.

Located next door to Marble Hill House is the **Orleans House Gallery**. The house that originally stood here was built in 1710 but demolished in 1926. All that remains is the Octagon Room, designed by James Gibbs. The outbuildings were opened as an art gallery in 1972, and include a display on the area's history.

During the summer you can take a ferry from Marble Hill House or the Orleans House Gallery to **Ham House**. (Alternatively you can take the tube or rail to Richmond station and then take bus Nos. 65 or 371.) This lovely red-brick building was built in 1610 and became famous in the 1670s when it was the home of the Duke of Lauderdale – a favourite of Charles II – who turned it into one of the country's most fashionable addresses. The grounds have been restored to their 17th-century grandeur.

Marble Hill House
Opening times: 10.30am–3.30pm Sat and Sun
(gardens open 6.30am–9pm daily)
Admission charges
https://www.english-heritage.org.uk/visit/places/
marble-hill-house
Tel: 020-8892 5115

Orleans House Gallery
Opening times: 10am–5pm daily; admission free
www.orleanshousegallery.org
Tel: 0208-831 6000

Ham House
Opening times: Noon–4pm daily; admission free
www.nationaltrust.org.uk/ham-house-and-garden
Tel: 020-8940 1950

Hampton Court ⑬

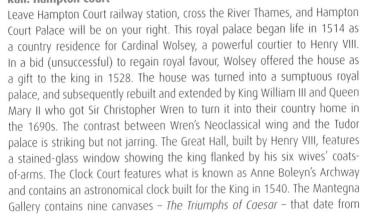

Rail: Hampton Court

Leave Hampton Court railway station, cross the River Thames, and Hampton Court Palace will be on your right. This royal palace began life in 1514 as a country residence for Cardinal Wolsey, a powerful courtier to Henry VIII. In a bid (unsuccessful) to regain royal favour, Wolsey offered the house as a gift to the king in 1528. The house was turned into a sumptuous royal palace, and subsequently rebuilt and extended by King William III and Queen Mary II who got Sir Christopher Wren to turn it into their country home in the 1690s. The contrast between Wren's Neoclassical wing and the Tudor palace is striking but not jarring. The Great Hall, built by Henry VIII, features a stained-glass window showing the king flanked by his six wives' coats-of-arms. The Clock Court features what is known as Anne Boleyn's Archway and contains an astronomical clock built for the King in 1540. The Mantegna Gallery contains nine canvases – *The Triumphs of Caesar* – that date from

Fountain Court, Hampton Court

BRACKEN DEC '10

1484–1505. The Chapel Royal was refitted by Wren, who kept its carved-and-gilded Tudor ceiling. Wren's cloistered Fountain Court is one of the building's highlights. An open-air internal courtyard, it is an exemplar of restrained Neoclassical elegance.

Hampton Court is a surprisingly intimate palace, and its riverside gardens are lovely to stroll in, with their radiating avenues, strategically placed fountains, lime trees and other more exotic species, as well as the longest herbaceous border in the world. The Pond Garden contains a charming, sunken garden with a pond that provided fish for Tudor banquets, while overlooking the river is the Banqueting House, where William III enjoyed intimate dinner parties. The gardens also contain a maze – which children love – and the Great Vine, planted in the 1760s, which used to produce up to 910 kilograms (2000 pounds) of grapes a year.

Hampton Court
Opening times: 10am–6pm daily
Admission charges
www.hrp.org.uk/hampton-court-palace
Tel: 020-6166 6000

Architectural Styles

BRACKEN JAN '11

Architectural Styles

Neoclassical

Classical architecture flowered in ancient Greece and Rome in the centuries before and after the birth of Christ. It disappeared with the fall of the Roman Empire, but was reinvented in the 16th century, first in Italy, by Andrea Palladio, and then throughout the rest of Europe and the world, thanks to architects such as Inigo Jones (1573–1652). Jones ended the practice that was common in England at the time of applying Neoclassical details simply as decoration. This had been the case during the Renaissance, which produced such oddly proportioned gems as the Jacobean Prodigy houses of Burghley, Longleat and Hatfield. Jones introduced Neoclassicism as an ideal, one that was governed by strict proportioning systems making use of the classical orders: Doric, Ionic, Corinthian, Tuscan and Composite. With his design for the Queen's House at Greenwich, he relied on the elegance of the building's proportions – especially that of wall to window – to make his architectural statements. He developed his ideas still further in the Banqueting House, Whitehall.

Neoclassical
(Banqueting House)

Gothic (Southwark Cathedral)

Gothic

Originating in northern France, the Gothic style rapidly spread to England thanks to the Norman invasion. Gothic architecture favoured soaring architectural features such as thin-ribbed ceilings, pointed arches, spires and delicate tracery, and evolved through a complex set of regional variants into a highly decorative style that was influential with artists, composers and manuscript illustrators. Its greatest glories are the medieval churches of northern Europe. In London, Westminster Abbey is a good example of the Gothic style, as is Southwark Cathedral.

With the revival of ancient Classicism during the Renaissance, the Gothic fell out of fashion, only to be revived in the 19th century, particularly in England. This was partly as a reaction to the unbroken centuries of Neoclassicism that had dominated stylistically, but also because of the influence of the hugely popular Gothic novel (such as William Beckford's *Vathek* and Horace Walpole's *Castle of Otranto*). A battle raged between Gothic Revival and Neoclassicism throughout the 19th century until new movements in architecture swept both away at the beginning of the 20th.

Arts and Crafts

Born out of the Gothic revival, the Arts and Crafts movement was widely influential in the late 19th-century. It attempted to re-establish skills and craftsmanship that were being lost to industrialisation and mass production. The writings of Pugin and Ruskin helped to popularise its ideals, but it was William Morris who took the most practical steps to re-establish industries along medieval manufacturing lines, which would retain truth to materials and make use of construction methods that adhered to the function and essence of their design – for example in textile-making and traditional wood-carving. The Norman Shaw Buildings at Whitehall are a good example of the style, and for an insight into Morris's efforts to revive traditional arts and crafts, visit the William Morris Gallery in Walthamstow (see the Further Afield chapter).

Byzantine

The Byzantine style experienced a fleeting vogue in London around the turn of the 20th century. Associated with the Byzantine Empire – established in modern-day Turkey circa 306 CE – its architecture is noted for luxurious use of colour, as is the case in Westminster Cathedral.

Art Deco

The Art Deco style was invented in Paris, taking its name from a 1925 exhibition on the decorative arts (*arts décoratifs*). It was the first global style to express the new aspirations and technical capabilities of the Modern era, and remained extremely-ly popular until the outbreak of World War II. Embracing a wide range of the arts – including architecture, photography, fashion, graphic design and film – its stream-lined elegance could be applied to a ciga-rette lighter just as easily as a luxury liner, to an apart-ment complex or the piano in its penthouse. Good examples of the style are the OXO Tower and BBC Broad-casting House.

Art Deco
(Broadcasting House)

Modernism

Modernism, or the Modern Movement, was a marriage of architecture and social theory that developed in the first decades of the 20th century, led by architects such as Walter Gropius, Ludwig Mies van der Rohe and Le Corbusier. It sought to eradicate any reference to history, as well as any hint of ornamentation, or indeed anything that these high-minded individuals thought might distract from the aim of using architecture to change society. In order for society to be better able to meet the rigours of the modern era, the Modern Movement embraced innovations from industry, which always emphasised efficiency and functional logic – the sheer starkness of their designs was all part and parcel of the ethos of the machine age. Modernist buildings commonly had blank glass facades, straightforward steel frames and simple concrete floors and interior supports. Floor plans were usually open, unencumbered by the traditional hierarchies of social space.

As the 20th century wore on, however, these designs, while immensely utilitarian and occasionally beautiful, began to be seen as sterile and unsympathetic to their local contexts; they also tended to exacerbate rather than ease social problems. Many of the buildings in the South Bank arts complex have been built in the Modernist style.

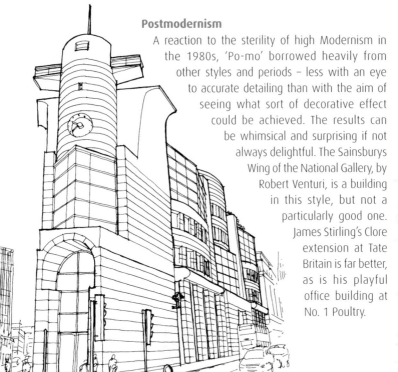

Postmodernism

A reaction to the sterility of high Modernism in the 1980s, 'Po-mo' borrowed heavily from other styles and periods – less with an eye to accurate detailing than with the aim of seeing what sort of decorative effect could be achieved. The results can be whimsical and surprising if not always delightful. The Sainsburys Wing of the National Gallery, by Robert Venturi, is a building in this style, but not a particularly good one. James Stirling's Clore extension at Tate Britain is far better, as is his playful office building at No. 1 Poultry.

Postmodernism
(No. 1 Poultry)

Architectural styles

High Tech

Also born out of high Modernism, the High Tech style sought to express a building's structure and technology by exposing it (e.g. the steel framing) and its services (e.g. the air ducts, electrical conduits, water pipes). Pioneered by Richard Rogers and Norman Foster, the style found its apotheosis in Rogers's design for Lloyd's of London. The building's services were all placed externally, to allow the interior to be as uncluttered as possible. This in a way echoed Gothic architecture's ethos of freeing up a building's interior by means of external buttresses and load-bearing spires – features that seem quaint and traditional today by virtue of their age, but that would have been incredibly high-tech in their day, seen against the restrained structural integrity of traditional Classical and Romanesque architecture.

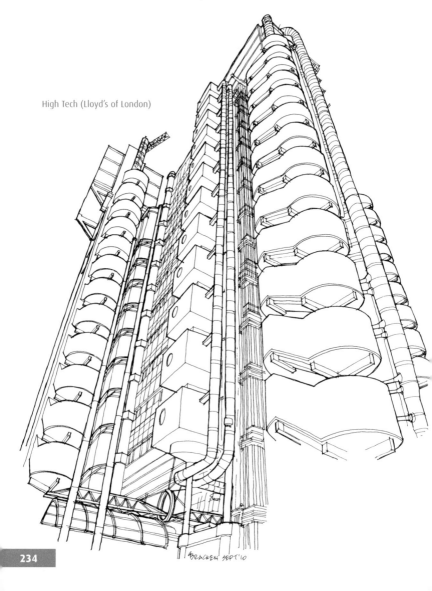

High Tech (Lloyd's of London)

GLOSSARY

apse A recess, usually semi-circular, projecting from an external wall.

arcade A long arched gallery or veranda, often open at only one side, formed by a series of arches supported by columns or piers.

arch Curved structure over opening.

Art Deco Style in art and architecture popular in the 1920s and '30s that drew inspiration from industrial elements.

Arts and Crafts Late 19th-century style that attempted to re-establish skills and craftsmanship threatened by industrialisation.

baluster A short post supporting a handrail.

Baroque Style of architecture in 16th- and 17th-century Europe which grew out of Renaissance Mannerism and evolved into the Rococo; typified by theatricality and exuberance of plan and decoration.

Brutalism Style of architecture popularised by Le Corbusier from about 1945, basically board-marked concrete, known as *béton brut*. Hugely influential with the architectural avant-garde for decades, particularly in Britain.

buttress Projecting wall support.

Byzantine Style associated with the Byzantine Empire (306–1453 CE), characterised by its rich use of colour and especially by square plans capped with round domes – a most unusual architectural quirk.

capital The head or topmost part of a column or pillar, often ornamental.

caryatid Column carved in the form of a female figure.

cella The part of a Greek or Roman temple enclosed within its walls.

chancel The part of a church that contains the altar and sanctuary and often the choir.

chapter house Building used for meetings, usually found in cathedrals, convents, and college chapels.

choir In larger churches, the place reserved for the choir or singers, sometimes screened.

Glossary

clerestory	The upper part of walls carried on arcades or colonnades in a church, higher than the external lean-to roofs, pierced with windows to allow light to penetrate.
colonnade	Row of columns (similar to an arcade).
column	A vertical supporting element.
Composite order	Grandest of the Roman orders, essentially an ornate version of the Ionic with two tiers of acanthus leaves under Ionic scrolls; it bears a strong resemblance to the Corinthian.
Corinthian order	Third of the Greek orders and fourth of the Roman; decorative, slender and elegant with two rows of acanthus leaves sprouting volutes or small scrolls.
cupola	Small dome.
dado	Surface of an internal wall like an extended pedestal all the way around a room (like a chair rail).
dentils	Small, square decorative blocks forming a moulding, especially under a cornice.
dome	A vaulted circular roof or ceiling.
Doric order	Classical order of architecture with distinct Greek and Roman varieties; simple in style, the Roman is less squat-looking than the Greek, always fluted but invariably without a base.
engaged column	A column embedded in or protruding from a wall.
faience	Earthenware covered with an opaque coating of enamel; essentially a type of glazed terracotta.
fascia	Long, flat board, usually wood, covering the ends of rafters.
fluting	Semi-circular channels that run vertically up and down a column or pillar.
frieze	Horizontal central band of Classical entablature, below the cornice and above the architrave.
gable	Triangular upper part of a wall at the end of a roof.
Georgian	Style of architecture in England during the reigns of George I to George IV (1714–1830), typified by restrained Neoclassicism, particularly the Roman and to a lesser extent the Greek; it also sometimes embraced more exotic elements from the Orient

Gothic	Style of architecture prevalent in Western Europe from the 12th to the 16th century and again in the 19th; its main features are pointed arches, delicate stonework and plenty of ornamentation.
Ionic order	Classical order of architecture, the second in Greek and the third in Roman; easily identified by its capital with its rolled-up scrolls; the Greek shafts are invariably fluted.
loggia	Open-sided arcade, often on an upper floor.
lunette	Panel on a wall under an arch or vault.
Mannerism	Architectural style of the late Renaissance, typified by use of Classical elements in unexpected or surprising ways.
motif	Design element that is repeated.
nave	The main body of a church, where worshippers sit.
Neoclassical	Style of architecture popular from the 17th century onwards and based on the architecture of ancient Greece and the Roman Empire; buildings are usually symmetrical, elegantly proportioned, and characterised by the generous use of columns and pillars.
Palladian	In the style of 16th-century Italian architect Andrea Palladio, who revived ancient Roman building styles and typologies; immensely influential for centuries.
peristyle	Colonnades surrounding a building or courtyard.
pilaster	An upright rectangular pier that looks like a pillar attached to a wall.
plinth	Plain continuous projecting surface under the base-mounting of a wall, pedestal or podium; the low plain block under a column or pillar in Classical architecture.
Pompeii Style	Colourful Neoclassical style of architecture that was popular from the mid-18th century onwards after the excavations of the Roman town that had been buried under volcanic ash since 79 CE.
portico	Roof supported by columns or pillars, usually forming an entrance.
Portland stone	A type of white limestone from Portland, in Dorset.
Queen Anne	Architectural style during the reign of Queen Anne (1702–14). A high point of the English Baroque, tempered by a Dutch influence that foreshadowed the restrained elegance of the Georgian.

Glossary

Regency	Style of architecture during the Regency of Prince George (1811–20), who later reigned as George IV from 1820 to 1830. Primarily Neoclassical, and very much influenced by the French Second Empire, it straddled the period when the purer Greek and Roman Neoclassicism turned to Gothic via a series of ever more exotic influences, such as Egyptian, Pompeiian, Chinese and Hindu architecture.
Romanesque	Architectural style in Europe from the 7th to 12th century (between the fall of the Roman Empire and the advent of Gothic), characterised by heavy stone masonry and small round windows and doors with coarsened Classical decorative features.
rose window	Circular window popular in Gothic architecture, especially in larger churches or cathedrals, usually subdivided by radial tracery forming a floral pattern of great complexity and beauty; also sometimes known as a marigold window or a wheel window.
scagliola	Imitation marble made of crushed gypsum, in use since Roman times.
terracotta	Hard unglazed pottery used in decorative tiles, urns and statuary, etc.
transept	Any large division at right angles to the main body of a building.
transom	Horizontal bar across a window or at the top of a door.
Tuscan order	One of the five Roman orders identified during the Renaissance; along with the Doric it is the simplest and least ornate.
Victorian	Style of architecture during the reign of Queen Victoria (1837–1901), characterised by what is often seen as an over-application of decoration.
Vitruvian	In the style of Roman architect Marcus Vitruvius Pollio, author of the only book of architecture to survive from the ancient world, *De Architectura*, which was hugely influential from the Renaissance onwards.

INDEX

Must See

18, 19, 36, 44, 45, 47, 51, 54, 58, 64, 66, 79, 84, 87, 90, 94, 96, 104, 110, 118, 119, 122, 123, 125, 131, 146, 148, 152, 154, 159, 175, 178, 182, 186, 187, 191, 198, 199, 213, 215, 218, 221

National Monument

18, 20, 25, 27, 35, 36, 40, 41, 44, 45, 47, 51, 58, 63, 64, 65, 66, 72, 74, 75, 77, 79, 84, 86, 87, 90, 91, 92, 93, 94, 96, 97, 102, 104, 108, 109, 110, 118, 119, 120, 122, 125, 131, 132, 134, 136, 137, 144, 148, 152, 154, 159, 162, 164, 170, 171, 182, 184, 186, 187, 189, 200, 209, 210, 214, 215, 216, 218, 221, 222, 224, 227

Good View

36, 47, 51, 58, 63, 64, 65, 66, 68, 72, 73, 74, 77, 79, 84, 86, 102, 104, 110, 118, 120, 131, 132, 135, 137, 146, 152, 171, 172, 173, 182, 184, 189, 193, 213, 215, 216, 218, 219

See At Night

44, 54, 58, 66, 72, 74, 79, 84, 110, 118, 122, 123, 125, 126, 130, 131, 134, 166, 178, 182, 187, 198, 201, 215, 216

Drinking

23, 47, 54, 60, 61, 62, 64, 72, 74, 107, 108, 110, 112, 113, 122, 123, 125, 130, 131, 132, 136, 147, 148, 158, 166, 170, 178, 182, 191, 193, 198, 211, 215, 217, 220

Eating

19, 22, 23, 47, 54, 60, 61, 62, 63, 64, 72, 74, 79, 89, 90, 107, 108, 110, 112, 113, 122, 123, 130, 131, 132, 136, 137, 147, 148, 158, 166, 170, 175, 178, 182, 191, 193, 198, 211, 215, 217, 220

Shopping

18, 19, 22, 23, 30, 47, 54, 60, 62, 63, 72, 74, 79, 92, 107, 108, 110, 112, 113, 121, 122, 123, 125, 130, 131, 136, 148, 150, 152, 154, 158, 166, 176, 178, 182, 191, 193, 198, 211, 215, 220